TRUST
PATIENCE
SURRENDER

Moments of Illumination and Grace

RTH Publishing

Red Tailed Hawk Publishing

P.O Box 3030, Sedona AZ 86340

TRUST PATIENCE SURRENDER

Copyright © 2013 by Kevin Westrich

Cover Design Peggy Sands, Indigo Disegno

Cover Red Tail Hawk Photo, Marv Collins

Interior Photos: Peggy Sands, Kevin Westrich, Mark Zyga,

Michael Iskowitz, Susie Schomacher, Loretta Hido

ISBN 13: 978-0-9892954-1-3

ISBN 10: 0-9892954-1-9

TABLE OF CONTENTS

FORWARD

"Let those who have eyes see, those who have ears hear."

All human beings are actually Spiritual Beings having a human experience. When one realizes this, life becomes really interesting and challenging.

Kevin's book is a very readable account of one man sharing his spiritual awakenings and the many ways Spirit has spoken to him. Each experience caused him to alter his perception of himself in relation to the meaning of his life. He has learned how to listen and trust unexpected guides and messengers.

Kevin manages to convey clearly the principles of living a spiritual life without using theological or thesis English. He is, in a real sense, "every man". His hope is to awaken and inspire others to begin or further their own lives. Every man or woman's story will be a unique adventure.

~ James Barnett
Swami Buddhananda

X

DEDICATION

To my reader please enjoy!

And

To those who have gone before me.

Virginia, my mother, and my brother, Kurt.

Also

To my friends who have walked with me.

There are too many to name.

You have my deepest gratitude.

Mitakuye Oyasin

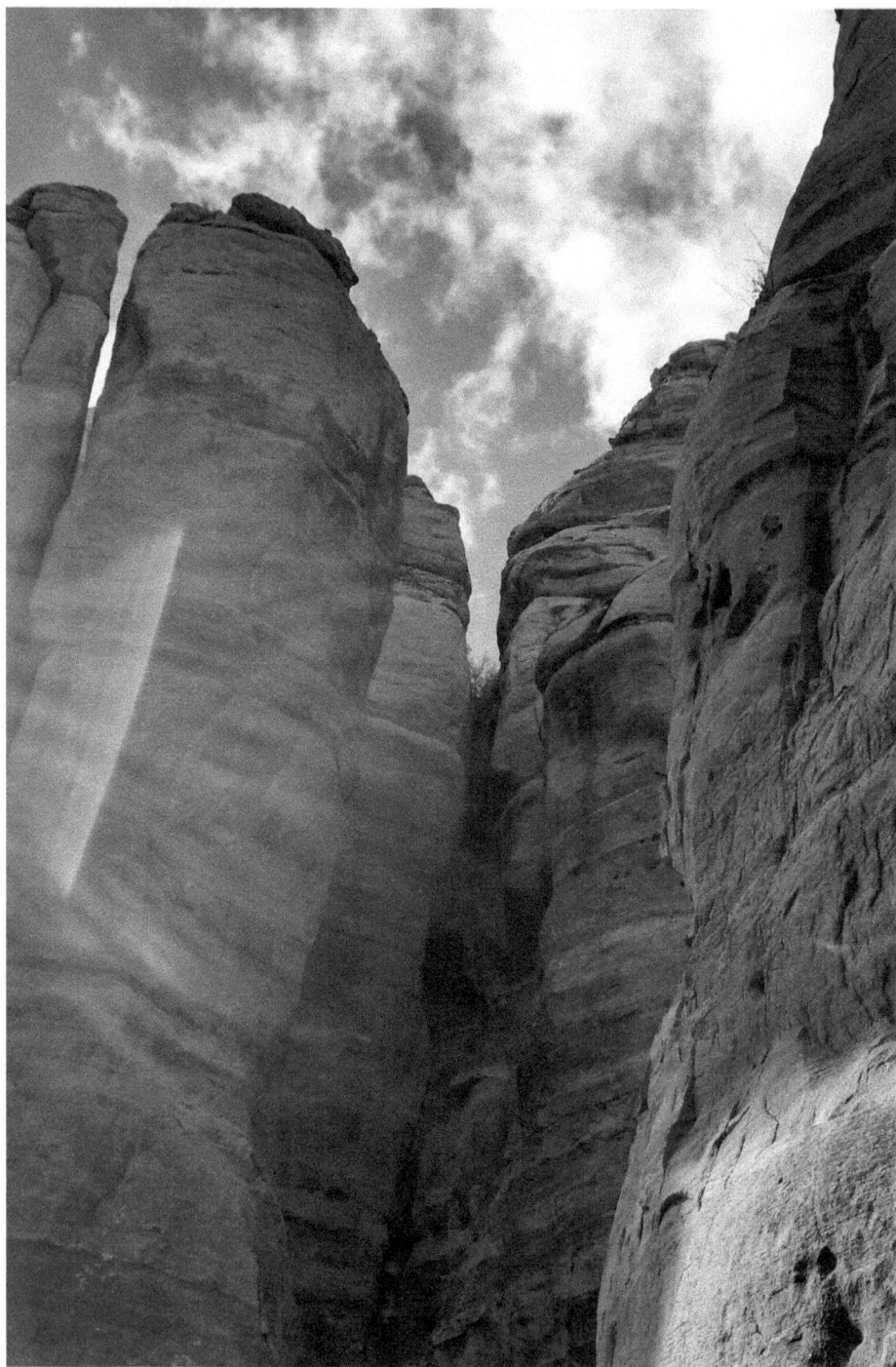

THANK YOU

Grandfather Morning Owl, your wisdom and kindness will always be remembered.

Keith W., your decades of conversations and inspiration kept me going.

Donna W., your unselfish love is sweet.

Keith D., your humor and hurling of knowledge has been priceless.

Laura, you took me further out to sea.

Dave B., your friendship kept me afloat.

Joel R., your friendship is always there.

Cassandra, your editing skills were heaven sent.

Peggy, your cover and layout allowed me to fly high.

Marv, thanks for the red-tail hawk photo.

INTRODUCTION

To my reader:

When you touch a place of deep being, you begin to let go, to trust.
When you release your frustration and anger, you begin to open to patience.
When you begin to forget yourself, you allow surrender.
Wisdom begins to surface, and the heart and mind gather as one, understanding the experience.
This is when you unclench your hands from the river bank, allowing yourself to be at one with the gentle flowing current, all the while, feeling the coolness of the waters.

I must confess that I began writing this book only after some time of resistance. Following a year or two of prodding from archangels, readers, and friends, I found the courage and commitment to put the words to paper.

The title came to me some years before my tobacco shop closed. As soon as they appeared in my thoughts, I wrote those magical three words – "Trust, Patience, Surrender" – on a little yellow note that I stuck to my cash register. I gazed at them many times. They were three words that I had asked God to reveal to me, not from an intellectual point of understanding but from an experiential one.

When I began to write this book, those magical three words appeared again in my thoughts.

You will encounter many examples of synchronicities, moments of grace, and experiences of suffering within this book. It will possibly be easy to compare yourself and your own experiences to the ones you are about to read. Please don't. It will only delay your own journey. My experiences have touched me deeply, and they have illuminated my own truths in understanding. You will have your own experiences that will reveal your truths, which are uniquely yours – and yours alone.

I do invite you to consider a couple of thoughts:

One, regardless of your spiritual or religious background, I invite you to deepen your own thoughts and desires around the topic of illumination or awakening, and to ask questions.

Two, open your mind and heart to something greater than what you currently understand. Miracles begin to happen when you decide to step outside of the box. One day these miracles will be so common that they will become the new normal state of being.

I have come to believe that we can only discover the capacity and meaning of our own uniqueness and divine nature in the context of our struggles and how we face the challenges that life presents to us. It is in going out, in search of something greater, that we eventually come back home to ourselves. That is when, I believe, we are able to come to the understanding that we are the gift to be given back to the world, that we are the temple, the synagogue, and the place of worship.

Remembering the Source that lives in all of us, and living it in the world, is a lifelong devotion.

It's also a joy.

CHAPTER 1

The Dark Night of My Soul

Soul: The immaterial essence, animating principle, or actuating cause of an individual life; the spiritual principle embodied in human beings, all rational and spiritual beings, or the universe; the moral emotional nature of human beings.
  ~ Merriam-Webster's Dictionary

I was living the high life.

I had a couple of expensive cars. I had a townhouse not far from Chicago's most prestigious neighborhood. I had a high-paying job managing retirement plans for enormous corporations such as Anheuser-Busch and Oprah Winfrey's Harpo Productions, Inc.

This was about eighteen years ago. Most people's minds were on OPEC, or on their shrinking wallets, or both. Yes, the U.S. economy was struggling, but I was in a field that was secure, growing, and profitable. (I'd always had a gift when it came to finding career paths. Somehow I'd always managed to enter sound industries in times of economic hardship for others.)

My days were consumed with work on 401(k)s and defined benefit plans; my nights were spent entertaining clients with lavish dinners. But during those rare moments when I had time to think about something other than work, I began to wonder if this corporate life wouldn't last much longer.

I was unsure about the future. And although I seemed to have an ideal job and career path, deep inside of me something was stirring – and stirring in a way that was self-sabotaging. I'd undermined myself before in other jobs, and I sensed that I was about to do it again.

And I did. It happened one evening at a company dinner with all my colleagues, plus a slew of young new trainees, the head of the trust department, and a corporate vice-president. I made the blunder that changed my life.

I was seated across from Ralph, the head of the corporate trust department, and beside one of the trainees, a friend I'd instructed in the nuances of the business. We were enjoying ourselves and drinking wine, a beautiful white wine from France. I was a connoisseur, and I knew that a characteristic of this particular wine was a slight taste almost like rubber. In the spirit of fun I said to the trainee, "This wine tastes like the inside of a Goodyear tire." Perhaps wanting to share the joke, the trainee caught Ralph's attention across from us and repeated my comment. Ralph's smile faded. Perhaps he thought I was insulting the company's choice of wine, or perhaps he thought I was too uneducated to appreciate a superior beverage – whatever he thought, he gave me a look of utter disdain. And deep inside I knew this meant trouble. But at the same time that moment was enlightening, for the look on Ralph's face confirmed my sense that it was time for me to leave that lifestyle. It was a small incident at the time, but it was the beginning of a major change.

Meanwhile, stressed with the pressures of corporate life, I'd been practicing Hatha yoga, meditating, and seeing an acupuncturist regularly. Yoga? Meditation? Acupuncture? These things were new to me at the time, but they made me feel good. I'd begun to believe that my coming life change was contained in the old saying, "When the student is ready the teacher appears." I believed that yoga, meditation, and acupuncture could help me decompress from the corporate world, and so I continued. I also began reading books on mysticism and spirituality.

And all these things were working. They seemed to be opening some new field of energy in my body. And they enabled me to feel really peaceful inside, rather than chaotic, and to become centered, rather than scattered. This was all new for me given the speed and stress of corporate life and its requirements to be productive.

The results of the yoga, acupuncture, and meditation became really clear to me that year on the day before Christmas. I was with a friend in line at a big liquor warehouse waiting to pay for my bottles of wine. While most people were impatient with the slow-moving line or just experiencing the typical holiday madness, I suddenly felt a sense of peace inside of me unlike anything I'd ever experienced. I could see people dashing around the store, running up and down the aisles, but the frantic holiday pace had no effect on me. I must have looked very calm, because my friend noticed the change in me. "What's going on with you?" she said. "You look, I don't know, peaceful."

I smiled and said, "Yes, I am."

And I knew I wanted to feel more of this peace on a regular basis.

The peaceful feelings ebbed and flowed during that holiday season. For amidst my new-found peace there was a problem. Like so many others, I'd gone through a bitter divorce, and my ex sometimes used our five-year-old son as a negotiating tool. I'd fly from Chicago to Saint Louis to spend time with him, only to find that I'd get to see him for a much shorter period than I'd expected, or that I wouldn't get to see him at all. That was rough.

One evening after an acupuncture session, my tears began to flow. I'd never been a man who cried, and now I couldn't understand what was going on. The acupuncturist said this was normal and that I should just let my emotions bubble up to the surface. Within twenty-four hours I was on my living room floor in a fetal position bawling my eyes out. What the heck was going on? I took my acupuncturist's advice and let the tears flow, but as I lay on the floor I was crying so hard that I was scared I'd never be able to stop. Nevertheless, I just let the emotions come out. I cried so hard that I had trouble breathing. But then, after about two hours of utter sobbing, still curled up in that fetal position, a deep silence came over me – one of those moments of quiet that seems to last for all of eternity.

I felt like I had just gotten rid of decades of repressed tears – emotions that had been locked away deep in my psyche for a very long time. At first I'd thought that the emotions were a result of not having my son for the holidays, but I soon realized something even bigger was going on, too, something much bigger than anything I could have imagined. Then all of a sudden, in the silence that followed my hours of weeping, an inner voice filled my mind and body with these words: "I want my mommy."

I was hearing from my own inner little boy deep within me. I had this need because my parents had been mostly absent at a critical point in my life. It wasn't their fault – they'd been busy and overwhelmed with caring for my brother Ken who died of leukemia – but nevertheless, my mother hadn't been there for me when I'd needed her most, and now I was releasing that pain of thirty years ago.

So I lay on the floor exhausted and numb for the next hour or so and continued to allow myself to experience any more feelings that wanted to come up.

When I was later able to get up off the floor and move around a bit, I called my friend Netti. During my hours of emotional release, I'd been terrified that I was either going nuts or having some kind of nervous breakdown. There was a history of emotional breakdowns in my family. Was I next? So I phoned Netti and explained what had happened. She congratulated me and said that what I'd gone through was spectacular, and she assured me that everything would be okay. I took comfort in her words because she was a true friend and a loving person.

After our phone call, I sat with my feelings and comforted myself as much as I could. And then came the sobering fact that in a few days I had to return to the corporate world – a world that was the antithesis of yoga, acupuncture, meditation, and expressing needs and emotions. But when I woke up the next day, I couldn't get out of bed. I felt my forehead to see if I had a fever. But no – there was no fever, no aches, and no pains. This was a malady that seemed to have no physical symptoms. I decided to allow whatever was happening to me to happen. It continued for nearly a week – I was almost totally bedridden. I could barely even get to the bathroom. When I needed to go there, I had to drop and drag myself across the floor.

A stack of my mystical and spiritual books sat by my bed on the nightstand. Now these books were feeding my soul. And I mean "feeding" almost literally, because during this time I ate nothing and could only drink water. I read several works by Merton, Moore, and Huxley, to name just a few. And it seemed as though a new doorway to my life was being opened.

As I reflected upon what was happening I realized that this was one of those experiences that I had read about called "The Dark Night of the Soul."

My life would never be the same. And somewhere deep inside of me this darkness, this unknowingness, was right where I was supposed to be. My whole world was being dismantled, and yet I was safe.

Simultaneously my world and any previous frame of reference began to change. My separation from it all expanded. Everything I'd thought to be true up until that point was dissolving. Career, money, status, the material world – these things no longer had me in their grasp. For me, the corporate life was coming to an end.

I came out of the experience realizing that I had to find a new way in the world. This was terrifying, and yet it was necessary. Leaving the business world that I knew so well was intimidating. And frightening thoughts raced through my mind: How can I make a decent living if I leave the corporate world? Where will I go? What will I do?

This was the opening of a doorway, the beginning of a spiritual journey that has continued ever since. And the journey would take me even further than I'd ever imagined into the dark recesses and shadowy realms of my psyche. For it would eventually bring me to the brink of death.

CHAPTER 2

SEDONA

The heart is an adventurer, the explorer of the mysteries, the discoverer of all that is hidden. The heart is always on a pilgrimage. It is never satisfied; it has an innermost discontent, a spiritual discontent. It never settles anywhere. It is very much in love with movement, with dynamism.
~ Osho

I knew I was on the threshold of an adventure. But I had no direction. I knew I would soon be leaving the corporate world, but I didn't know where I was going. Or what I'd do when I got there. So I took some time off from work to clear my head and to see what non-corporate opportunities might be available to me.

A friend suggested I go visit her mother's bed and breakfast in Tucson. Bed and breakfast? I was used to luxury hotels with room service. But I thought, "Why not give it a try?" My friend enthralled me with accounts of how the Arizona weather would be warm and sunny. Meanwhile, Chicago in the winter of 1996 was even colder than usual, with its subzero weather and chilling winds.

A few days later I boarded a plane for Arizona with only a small carry-on bag. I felt such a feeling of freedom – a freedom of leaving a life that no longer fit me. I didn't know where I would end up, but that didn't matter. Something bigger was in store. I relaxed into these feelings and fell asleep on the plane.

My flight had a short stopover in Phoenix before arriving in

Tucson, and as we touched down I awoke from a deep sleep and heard a voice inside my head saying, "Get off the airplane." And without further questioning, that was exactly what I did.

Entering the terminal, I wasn't sure what I was going to do so I asked Spirit to show me the way. I walked through the crowds and thoughts raced through my mind about why I'd been instructed to deplane. Was the flight going to be delayed? Was I being saved from an impending plane crash?

Still needing to get to Tucson, I stepped over to the car rental counters. After waiting in line for quite a while, my turn finally came. But when I stepped up to the counter, a wave of nausea washed over me. The clerk looked confused as I said, "Thanks anyway, but I don't think I'm supposed to drive to my destination" and walked away. There was a shuttle bus right outside the airport, and I thought maybe this was how I'd get to Tucson. But the nausea returned as I made my way toward the shuttle ticket counter.

Still wandering in the airport, I saw a board listing local hotels. The nausea abated as I read the names of the hotels, so I assumed I'd be spending the night in Phoenix. Thirty minutes later I was checked into a room at the Holiday Inn. By now I was hungry, and fortunately there was a restaurant right across the street.

It was an English-style pub called George and the Dragon. I was early for dinner, so I easily found a table, sat down, opened my journal, and began to write. After a while, the chef emerged through the kitchen doors, came over to my table, and started up a conversation. After I ordered my fish and chips, he asked what I was doing in Phoenix. I explained what had just happened on the airplane and at the airport. And no sooner had those words left my mouth than he began raving enthusiastically about the place where he'd spent the previous weekend with his girlfriend. It was a magical place, he said – so magical that he'd been moved to propose to his girlfriend. The whole experience had made him cry. "Cry!" he said. "Can you imagine? I'm an Englishman – we're famous for being stalwart. Stiff upper lip and all that, you know. I never cry. But I did. That's what a magical place it is!" And then he looked me right in the eye and added, "That's where you're going."

With certainty in his voice he exclaimed, "You're going to Sedona."

I looked at him. By now, I was very accepting of the strange information I'd been receiving lately, so I just smiled and said, "Okay!" We talked a bit more, and as more people began to arrive for dinner, he said farewell and returned to the kitchen.

Later, as I ate my fish and chips, I opened my journal and began to write again. Eventually two young ladies approached me and started a conversation. I'd just begun to tell them my story when they interrupted me and nearly screamed, "You're going to Sedona!" If I hadn't been convinced before, by now I was certain that this would be the next stop on my journey.

The following morning I checked out of the Holiday Inn, cancelled my B & B reservation in Tucson, and headed to another car rental company. This time there was no nausea. I rented a red Mustang convertible. Soon I was off!

The dry heat blew across my face as I headed for Sedona. I was so full of joy that I stopped several times on the side of the highway just to bask in the sun. After a few hours, I saw the turnoff to Sedona, and I headed west on Highway 179. Then I rounded a turn and there they were: the magical red rocks! I was so overwhelmed that I had tears in my eyes and an inner knowledge that this was home. Feelings rose up in me that seemed both strange yet natural. The place was familiar, as if I'd been here before. Instinctively, I knew this was the womb of mother earth and that here, I would be nurtured.

At the time, I had a theory about why the red rocks made me feel so at home. A few months earlier my father had told me, my brother, and my sisters that the man we'd known as our maternal grandfather wasn't really a biological relative. I'd loved him my grandfather, and it didn't matter whether he was really my grandfather or not. But my father went on to tell us about our biological grandfather. He was a Cherokee from Tiptonville, Tennessee. This clarified a lot. For one thing, it explained why my oldest sister, Denise, was brown skinned with high cheekbones and jet black hair and why her two children looked as if they'd just come off a reservation. It also explained why I'd always been so intrigued by Indian culture. My father's story was confirmed when my sister Dahlia and I went to visit our Cherokee family in Tiptonville. We met our biological aunts, uncles, and cousins, including a colorful aunt named Elsie who gave us a lot of information about our grandfather and our heritage.

So now here I was in Arizona, a state known for its Native American heritage. As I had driven up to Sedona, I'd felt whisked back to another time. As I'd passed signs for places with Western names like "Dead Horse Creek" and "Bloody Basin," I'd felt like I was back in the Wild West – and that this was where I belonged.

I spent a week among Sedona's red rocks hiking, sleeping, and relaxing in the cool waters of the creek. The time flew by, and I dreaded having to return to Chicago. I made new acquaintances very quickly, and I met a couple, Tom and Marti Norris, who had a company called TN Productions that produced videos. We formed a friendship, and they asked me to come and work for them, writing, scripting, and producing local TV commercials. The money wasn't great, but the important thing was that the job was based in Sedona. But I wasn't yet completely ready to let go of my life back in Chicago, so I told them I'd have to think about it.

Back home a week later, Chicago seemed pale in comparison to the excitement of my visit to the "Wild West" and the beauty of Sedona. So several weeks later, once again I was on a plane bound for Arizona. I wasn't yet ready to cut the ties to the city life I'd built, but I couldn't resist the allure of Sedona.

The second trip was even better than the first, and again, when the time came to depart I was filled with regret. I really didn't want to leave. Yet I still hadn't made a firm decision to move, and I still hadn't given Tom an answer about his Sedona job offer.

I returned to Chicago yet again, and a few weeks later I felt a deep disturbance about moving. Every nerve ending in my body felt raw, and the tips of my fingers seemed to be peeling away. It was nearly impossible to function in my daily life.

One evening at dinner I told some friends about my trips. They all agreed that I should quit my corporate job and move. They spent most of the evening encouraging me to go. Still, I was uncertain.

That night as I walked the few blocks from the restaurant back toward my home alone, I wondered how I could possibly leave a life that was so stable and lucrative. How could I go alone to a strange place in another part of the country? I was used to city life – Sedona was a small town. I was living in a humid city on one of the Great Lakes – Sedona was in the arid desert. True, it wasn't as blistering hot in the summer as Phoenix or Tucson, but the climate was completely different than what I was used to. In addition, the job I'd been offered paid barely a fraction of my corporate earnings.

As these thoughts plagued me, all of a sudden I blurted out loud: "God, if Sedona is to be my new home, you must show me an unmistakable sign. Do that, and I will go."

No sooner had I said these words, than I rounded the corner and walked by an art gallery that I'd passed many times but never really noticed. This time, however, I noticed it. Far inside the gallery on the back wall was a painting. It seemed to be glowing like a beam of light. I pressed my face against the picture window and there it was: a small, twelve-inch-by-twelve-inch painting of Sedona's famous Cathedral Rock.

This was it: the sign I'd asked for.

I moved to Sedona just a few weeks later.

CHAPTER 3

The Move

As your attachment to the world diminishes, your spiritual knowledge will increase.

~ Ramakrishna

Over the past eighteen years I've heard many stories from people who were drawn to Sedona, as I was, from all over the country and even from around the world. Perhaps my favorite is the story of a truck driver who passed through town and was so moved by the landscape that he phoned his wife and told her to pack up their belongings because he'd found their new home. Many people have received a calling from somewhere deep inside their psyches and moved here without knowing a thing about this mystical place.

And yet Sedona can be an unforgiving place for those who come for selfish or superficial reasons. People in Sedona refer to the town as "her" and not "it," because she has a spirit all her own. She can rouse the darkness in your soul and challenge you to clear and heal it. As an old saying goes, "If you are meant to live in Sedona, she will welcome you with open arms; if you aren't ready, she'll chew you up and spit you out." Sedona is a magical place whose mysteries are bound only by one's own creative and spiritual nature. The Hopi, Navaho, and Yavapai Apache nations will tell you that Sedona is a place to visit only. Do your ceremonies, they'll say, and then leave the land of the red rocks: it is too powerful a place to live in.

Yet if you want to make a local Native American laugh, just tell them about Sedona's sacred power places. White people call these vortexes or vortices. The term "vortex" was coined in the 1980s by a woman named Page Bryant. A vortex, she said, is an area in Sedona with highly concentrated energies that are conducive to prayer, meditation, and healing. Bryant identified several such places in Sedona and said some vortices have male energies, some have female energies, and one contains both. But the local Native Americans find the idea ridiculous. They believe that all of Sedona is sacred and powerful; this is why their peoples from far and wide have visited the area for many generations. Some indigenous nations even believe that Sedona was the birthplace of their people.

From a scientific standpoint, although the rocks of Sedona seem predominantly red, by volume the rocks are ninety-six percent sandstone and silicone quartz, which are light tan. Silicone quartz is what capacitors are made of, and capacitors are used in conducting electricity and in electronic devices. So Sedona consists primarily of the material that might make up a huge capacitor. The remaining four percent is iron oxide, which provides the red color. The iron oxide covers each grain of sand with the color red, the way the skin covers an apple.

Now that I've lived here for many years I can attest to one truth about Sedona: if you are called to live here, your life will change – and change drastically.

Once I had made up my mind to leave Chicago, I was permeated with feelings of excitement knowing I'd be entering a new region, a new town, and a new life. I had a sense of being an explorer as I packed my small suitcase. I prepared most of my belongings for pick-up by a moving company – I wanted to travel light during the drive to Sedona. All that I really needed were the clothes on my back, a few changes of clothing, and odds and ends like my birth certificate and my military discharge papers.

I arrived in Sedona ready to accept my new job with TN Productions, writing and producing local TV commercials and advertising brochures. As soon as I got settled, I contacted the owners, only to find out that no job was awaiting me. Marti, the wife and co-owner, had just had a heart attack, and Tom had decided to scale back the business until she was fully recovered.

I was sympathetic, of course, but I was also stunned. Here I was with no job and limited savings that I would exhaust within a few months.

But instead of looking for employment right away, for the first few weeks I decided just to relax and decompress from the hectic pace of the corporate world that had been my life for years. I bought some camping gear and some books by spiritual and metaphysical authors, and I set up a tent in the National Forest in Yavapai County.

There in the sun, with my feet in the crystal clear waters of Oak Creek, I lounged on large basalt and rounded river rocks that had drifted down from the five-hundred-foot canyons above. I spent my days in reading, prayer, and meditation. On several occasions while I was camped, I did three-day water fasts. Sometimes I asked the spiritual forces that had brought me to Sedona to reveal what I was to do next. Some days I'd ask with utter calm and peacefulness, but at other times I'd be afraid, not knowing what might lie ahead.

However, as good luck would have it, Tom from TN Productions soon contacted me to say that his wife was recovering nicely, and that they were ready for me to come on board. Although I was excited, I was also anxious as I'd never written a TV commercial let alone a program for PBS. But over the next year I put my corporate and sales experience to work, writing local TV ads and copy for four-color printed brochures.

Meanwhile, as bad luck would have it, the moving company was holding my belongings in Phoenix and refusing to release them to me. We had agreed on a moving fee, and I had the agreement in writing, but now the company demanded three times the amount of the original quote. The movers wouldn't budge from their stance, so I contacted the offices of the attorneys general in Arizona and Illinois and eventually sued the movers in court. I won the judgment, but when I asked the magistrate what to do next, he just gave me a wry smile and said, "Good luck." I took that to be an ominous sign.

For six months, all of my belongings – everything I owned – had been held hostage and now, even with a judgment against the moving company, I still didn't have my things. Finally I was so exhausted from the whole experience that I just looked up at the sky and shouted, "God, either bring me my belongings or take them away!"

Be careful what you wish for.

Within forty-eight hours, I got a phone call from a man at the moving company who said, "I'm sending via overnight express the paperwork and the storage keys to you. You must get your things out of storage tomorrow because we are going bankrupt." The next morning I received the keys and the paperwork, just as he'd promised. This was great; things were moving forward, and I was stoked! I rented a fifteen-foot truck to move my things to Sedona and headed down to Phoenix. I arrived at the storage place, presented the paperwork at the front office, and asked which storage room contained my belongings. The clerk instructed me to go down the hall and to the left. I found my unit, but when I tried to put the key into the lock, it didn't fit.

I went back to the front desk, again showed my paperwork, and asked why my key wouldn't fit. The clerk did some checking and after a few minutes he said, "We auctioned off all of your things two weeks ago."

I was speechless. Tears welled up in my eyes. Almost everything I owned was now gone. It wasn't the material possessions that I cared about, but things like my son's first teddy bear and all of my family photos. They were all gone forever.

My mood turned quickly from sadness to rage. Soon I had the storage facilities regional director on the phone. "How dare you! How can you do this to me?" I screamed into the phone. But she just answered calmly, "We did everything legally." For a storage fee of $67 that I hadn't even known about, every belonging that meant anything to me had been auctioned to strangers.

I trudged back to the empty fifteen-foot truck and headed back to Sedona. I felt numb. But during the trip I tried to center myself, and I asked the question, "What am I to learn from this experience?" For the next two hours I pondered this question, and finally I realized that the message was that if I could resist becoming attached to worldly things, even those with personal and sentimental value, I'd be all right.

Knowing that the lesson was non-attachment, despite the pain, a sense of peace washed over me.

CHAPTER 4

MATTHEW

*Language . . . has created the word "loneliness" to express the pain of
being alone. And it has created the word "solitude" to express the glory of
being alone.*
  ~ Paul Tillich

As if losing all of my belongings was not enough, a few months later,
I experienced another painful loss. And this time, I lost a person.
During my year in Sedona I'd been attending Unity Spiritual Center.
The pastor, a man named Matthew, had become like a father to me,
if not even more than that. I respected and admired him. All my life
I had sought a father figure – but not some "macho man." Instead I
was looking for someone who encompassed both masculine and feminine qualities, someone who could be open and receptive while being
strong and constructive. And Matthew had all of these qualities.

This was the first time in my life that I'd actually begun to trust a
man, particularly one in a place of power.

The last time I had encountered a powerful man like this was in
my early twenties. In the midst of a traumatic divorce, I met a priest
who was involved with parishes all over the world. He offered me the
opportunity of a lifetime, which was to go to the Wharton School of
Business, one of the best business schools in the country. But there
was a catch: he wanted sexual favors in return. This was something
I couldn't do. Now, in spite of that terrible experience, I had bonded

with Matthew. He was a large man, taller than six feet four, but he displayed a gentleness at times that truly helped me. He had a magnetic presence and an appealing voice that would emanate throughout the sanctuary when he spoke. But the quality that I most valued in him was his balance of energies. At times he could be receptive, just listening quietly; at other times he would be direct and would frankly speak his mind.

I had attended many of his classes over the past year, and I was pleased to feel my trust deepening.

But now he announced that he was moving to Walnut Creek, California, to head up the Unity facility there.

I was devastated. I felt like he was abandoning me. Thoughts like "How could he leave now just when I was beginning to trust him?" filled my head. And I wasn't the only one who felt this way. The whole parish seemed shocked. Nevertheless, Matthew left us and went to Walnut Creek.

Meanwhile, in the midst of my emotional turmoil and feelings of abandonment, my employer was waffling whether to keep me on board. The tiny production company had begun as an operation for local TV, and now I was trying to take them into the world marketplace. They let me know they were scared and didn't think they were prepared to begin creating shows on an international level.

We had an upcoming meeting with some executive producers in Los Angeles, and my employers said that after this meeting they'd let me know whether they'd keep me with their company. I agreed to give them the time they needed to think about the expansion, and I decided that while they thought things over, I'd go visit Matthew in California. I called to say I wanted to see him. He told me he was glad to hear from me and was looking forward to seeing me again.

I packed a few things and left very early the following morning, which was a Friday, for Walnut Creek. I travelled for the next eighteen hours, and as I drove, I realized how anxious I was about what was going on at my job. The husband-and-wife team wasn't ready to expand the business, but I was. In spite of my discomfort, however, I was confident that Matthew, my surrogate father, would have all the answers I needed.

When I was four hours away from Walnut Creek, I stopped to call Matthew to let him know I was on my way.

By the time I arrived, I was exhausted after the long drive from Sedona to Walnut Creek. After what seemed like an eternity in the car, I finally pulled into the parking lot of Matthew's parish on Saturday evening. It was dark as I walked up to the door, knocked, and waited. A woman in her fifties answered the door and asked, "May I help you?"

I almost collapsed from fatigue, but managed to say, "I'm here to see Matthew."

Apparently, he hadn't told her I was coming, because she looked very surprised to see me. "He's gone out to dinner with some friends," she said, "I'm not sure when he's coming back." Then she asked, "Was he expecting you?"

I was shocked, but I composed myself enough to say, "I just drove eighteen hours to see him. I called four hours ago to let him know I was coming."

She replied, "I'm sure he'll be happy to talk with you tomorrow at the Sunday service, but I have no way of reaching him tonight."

I thanked her as she closed the door. Before I made it back to the car, there in the darkness I collapsed to the ground and began to cry. Thoughts of disappointment raced through my head: "How could Matthew have forgotten me?" I wondered. Too upset to drive, I spent the next hour wandering in the church gardens in the dark, crying and assessing my place in the world. Was I such a worthless creature that I was so easily forgotten by the man I admired most in the world? The pain of this question was almost unbearable. I finally calmed down enough to drive to a hotel to get some rest.

The next morning I went to the Sunday service, and I stood in line with the others to greet Matthew. When he saw me, he looked extremely embarrassed. He quietly asked me to go to the church office and wait for him there. Soon he came into his office and sat on the sofa beside me. He asked, "What do you need and what can I do?" And then he hugged me to his chest.

I began sobbing. He held me for some time. I had considered going to a monastery to study, and when I regained my composure I said, "I want to go to a monastery to rest." His assistant made a few calls and recommended one in Santa Rosa. I thanked him for his time, got into my rental car, and headed toward the monastery.

However, as I drove to the monastery that Matthew's assistant arranged for me in Santa Rosa, I realized that this wasn't the path that I was to take. So I turned the car around and headed back to Sedona.

During my drive home I came to an important realization: No one in this world could give me a sense of peace. Not even Matthew. I had to find it on my own. I had a connection to God and to myself, and that was all.

I had experienced the clear and direct awareness that, as they say, "We come into this world alone and we will leave it alone." God and myself would have to be enough for me. All other experiences would be icing on the cake.

CHAPTER 5

THE SEDONA HEALING CENTER VORTEX

If someone is able to show me that what I think or do is not right, I will happily change, for I seek the truth, by which no one was ever truly harmed. It is the person who continues in his self-deception and ignorance who is harmed.

~ *Marcus Aurelius*

The vortices of Sedona are powerful, of course, but we should never forget the equally profound power of the red rocks. Since coming here I've learned that the color red can have an intense effect on the human psyche. It's no coincidence that stop lights, stop signs, and danger signs are this color. Numerous studies have indicated that the color red can evoke emotions including aggressiveness and anger, while the color blue promotes a soothing, cooling effect. Another thing I've learned is that being in this semi-arid climate, Sedona's quiet beauty and sparse vegetation can bring one to a place of quiet inside within oneself. And for many, that can be a scary place, at first.

On my first visit to the Hopi mesas not far from Sedona and to the community of Hotevilla and Oraibi, I learned that Oraibi is the oldest continuously inhabited community in America, having been lived in for over 900 years. It was founded at roughly the same time that the indigenous peoples inhabiting the areas bordering Sedona abandoned their communities. As I explored the seemingly desolate mesas and wandered through the Hopi Cultural Center,

I wondered how anyone could survive in such a place.

One day not long after I first came to Northern Arizona, I pulled my car over to the side of the road and sat down on the edge of one of the cliffs. As I sat and quieted my mind I felt a strange stillness that was not comforting, but that shattered my level of comfort. It was complete silence; not even the wind was stirring. After several minutes the only thing I could feel or sense was the beating of my own heart. This was a bit scary at first, and I had to pinch one of my arms to see if I still was alive. And then a smile came across my face as I remembered that such a silence does exist. During my time in the corporate world and the big city back East, I'd somehow forgotten this.

Over the years it's been fascinating to talk with people about their experiences with Sedona and her places of power. I've encountered folks who, when the topic of the vortices comes up, will say, "I'm out of here – you people are all nuts." But others will say, instead, "I've felt the power, and my life will never be the same."

I should add that when I first came to Sedona I was skeptical about such supernatural and metaphysical stuff. But gradually I began to open up to the notion that such things could exist.

So it was with a semi-open mind that, on a warm summer's afternoon, my friend Katherine and I went to a place called the Sedona Healing Center. It was owned by a man named Jacques. When we arrived at the Center we were met by Jacques himself, a likeable guy with blond hair. As we walked around the property with him, he shared his story of how he'd come to this particular part of Sedona.

He pointed to a rock and said, "This was where I meditated for several years prior to purchasing the property." He said it was a vortex and that it emitted powerful energy. Not knowing much about vortices at the time, I was intrigued and asked him to tell me more about these energies.

As a way of answering, he took Katherine and me inside the Center. He told us to go upstairs and see if we could feel anything unusual. He instructed us each to go up alone and explore, and to sit down where we believed we felt something.

I decided to go first. Upstairs alone, I walked around very slowly and tried to feel something. I didn't know what to look for, so I tried listening intently, thinking the energy might be something I could hear. I also tried to tune in with my body to see if I could feel any kind of vibrations.

When I reached an area to the left of the stairs, I began to feel lightheaded.

As I said earlier, Sedona consists primarily of the material that might make up a huge capacitor. I know perhaps more than most people about capacitors, because when I was in the Navy I was a radioman. That means I worked with electronics equipment such as transmitters and receivers that communicated our ship's messages to the military. One thing I came to know very well was that large transmitters and antennas can put out enough energy to make the hair stand up on the back of your neck and to create a physical sensation inside your heart as if it is skipping a beat.

Now I began to feel the way I'd sometimes felt years earlier in the Navy as a radioman. Still lightheaded, I sat down on the floor, and as I did, the hair was standing up on the back of my neck. My heart felt as if it was skipping a beat. I was feeling increasingly disoriented, and so I quickly went back downstairs.

Now it was Katherine's turn. Without speaking to me first, she headed up the stairs. After several minutes of walking around, she called down to us. I looked up the stairwell, and I could see her sitting just inches away from where I myself had sat just minutes earlier.

After she came back downstairs, we explored the rest of the center. Finally, we thanked Jacques for his hospitality, and feeling much less skeptical, we headed for home.

Given my own experiences over the past eighteen years, I've learned the advantages of being open-minded and accepting over being closed-minded and skeptical. If you are open to new experiences and new possibilities with an open mind and heart, much will be revealed to you.

CHAPTER 6

Manifesting Cuba

Manifesting is a lot like making a cake. The things needed are supplied by you, the mixing is done by your mind, and the baking is done in the oven of the universe.
~ Stephen Richards

In 2006, the self-help film *The Secret* made a huge splash around the world and attracted the attention of celebrities such as Oprah Winfrey and Larry King. For those who haven't seen it, the film is about how one's desires can be achieved – or "manifested" – by focusing positively on an outcome. This philosophy is also sometimes called the "Law of Attraction," which holds that positive feelings and thoughts can attract or "manifest" positive results. So over the last few years there's been a lot of talk and energy about this idea of "manifesting." I experienced this phenomenon multiple times a decade before *The Secret.* And I continue to experience it. Call it divine timing or synchronicity, but I've seen things become manifested in my life as a result of my own positive focus. Today, my attitude toward manifesting involves not wanting material things specifically, but asking, "Bring that which is for my greatest good and in ways I will understand." But this wasn't always my position. I have realized that I must wrap the request with emotions from my heart. This is extremely important!

Having worked for so many years in the corporate world, my original attitude was like a child's. I demanded what I wanted: a flashy car, a stunning condo, more money, etc. But eventually those things lost their luster. Now I believe that I don't always know what will be for my greatest good, so I've come to rely on living in the present moment and paying attention to the signs and the feedback I receive from the universe. When things do appear, I think of them as manifested.

Fifteen years ago in Sedona I began manifesting things without even knowing what I was doing. For example, at one point I would fall asleep at night with an image of a Harley-Davidson Fat Boy motorcycle and with the amount of $150,000 in my mind. I would also envision a loving relationship. As fate would have it, my visions became reality within a matter of weeks.

At one time I had a retail cigar store, and a lot of customers had special requests. I'd make a note of what each person wanted, and I'd usually either search for and find the item or it would somehow just arrive unordered in a shipment of other things. The problem was that sometimes once I had the item, I had no way to contact the customer. So I would stand at my cash register and hold the person in my thoughts, sending the message that I had what he wanted. And more often than not the customer would show up at the shop a day or two later − sometimes even on the same day. Often the person would say something like "I've been thinking about you" or "You've been on my mind, so I decided to stop in."

Another story of manifesting involves meeting a man from Huntington Beach, California. On a beautiful sunny day in June, I was enjoying a stogie on the patio of my store, but I was a little depressed because my home stereo had just broken down. It was a good system that would cost thousands of dollars to replace. As I sat smoking, a man pulled up in a big Hummer, got out, walked over, and said he was looking for some exotic cigars.

I asked some questions about exactly what he wanted, and then I told him I could get the expensive items he wanted and could ship them to him. He was ecstatic! I offered him a cigar and as we sat smoking he explained that he'd made it big in the stock market investing in penny stocks and had become a multi-millionaire almost overnight. He also said he had a design firm that built professional stereo equipment. Finally, he asked rather hesitantly if I might be willing to barter the cigars for a stereo system. Would I ever!

A week later the cigars I'd ordered for him arrived, and I drove to Huntington Beach to drop them off and to visit his warehouse. Not only did he give me some great stereo equipment for my home, he suggested I needed a system for my shop, as well. And he gave that to me, too, as part of the bargain.

But perhaps my greatest manifestation experience took place before Christmas in 2002. Because I was in the cigar business, I had an interest in Cuba. I was attracted to the culture, the music, and the overall mystique of the island; plus it was the home of the world's greatest cigars. My dream had nothing to do with tobacco, however; instead, I wanted to go to Cuba to work with children in the hospitals there. I had mentioned this to my sales rep who visited the shop occasionally, and he suggested that I telephone a man named Luke Richards in Austin. Luke was a director of the Amistad Cuba Foundation, a group that does humanitarian work in Cuba.

I phoned and had a long conversation with Luke, and I explained my interest in Cuba in general and in humanitarian efforts in particular. I told him I'd like to go to Cuba some day and help out in a hospital. He appreciated my enthusiasm, he said, but no one besides doctors and other medical professionals was allowed to participate in the program. I promised to support the organization by sending some money for the children, which I did. And the organization stayed in my mind – along with my slight disappointment that I'd never be able to help in a hands-on way.

A few months later, on a cold night in December just as I was about to lock up the store, a man appeared. He introduced himself as Kyle. His wife was sick with severe allergies and she was back in the room where they were staying, at the Enchantment Resort. He was bored, he said, and was just looking around when he saw my cigar shop. I invited him in, and we talked for some time about Cuban cigars, the Cuban culture, and other aspects of the island. Without mentioning its name, he said he was part of an organization that was hosting a benefit dinner to raise funds for humanitarian aid to Cuba. I offered to donate some items to be sold at the dinner: some cigar lamps (handcrafted specialty items made from high-quality wooden cigar boxes) as well as some cigars. He was very appreciative.

We talked some more, and soon he was telling me more about this organization, and how and why he had founded it. I could hardly believe my ears when he said its name: the Amistad Cuba Foundation. He was the founder and president! I excitedly told him I'd spoken with one of the directors, Luke Richards of Austin, just a few months before, and that I'd donated some money to the cause. Kyle said he hadn't heard about this, but the organization had a lot of donors, so he was unlikely to hear about each one. He thanked me, and eventually our conversation drew to a close, and he returned to his hotel to check on his sick wife.

Several days later he called to tell me how great the lamps looked and how much he appreciated my donations. We talked a bit more, and finally he said, "You may come with us on our February mission to Cuba."

After he hung up, I just sat there with a smile on my face and the knowledge that if I put my thoughts out into the universe, and if I fully believe that what I want is possible and is for the greatest good, my dreams and wishes will be fulfilled.

CHAPTER 7

Totems

The central theme of the kachina [religion] is the presence of life in all objects that fill the universe. Everything has an essence or a life force, and humans must interact with these or fail to survive.
  ~ Wright Barton

A totem is a distinctive and venerated emblem or symbol. Totems have always been a very powerful aspect of Native American cultures, tribes, and clans. Typically, totems are sacred deities and or animal spirits that assist and protect individuals on their journey through life. They are a gift when the individual is ready to receive them or after the person has gone through some rite of passage or ceremony.

My teacher is Grandfather Morning Owl. He isn't actually Native American. He was first of the Vedanta religion. He studied comparative religions for twenty-eight years. At the end of the twenty-eight years he was called by his internal voice to leave his position as head of the San Diego Vedanta Center, and to enter the world doing healing work that included Native American ceremonies around the world. He also created a program of healing modalities for helping those who were dying to release any emotional baggage so they could pass through the dying experience peacefully. He has been an essential part of my life for the last ten years, and he's not just a teacher, he's my friend. Many times in the past I asked him what my power animal was, and his response was always the same: "It will come to you. Just be patient."

During these years I also prayed to God to reveal the animal that would speak to me and guide me. Sometimes I'd do this as I smoked cigars in my shop, knowing that my prayers were being sent in the smoke that curled its way up to the heavens. I also went into the Yavapai and Coconino National Forests many times to look up to the sky and ask for my animal totem to be revealed to me.

Then one day I was talking with my friend Tora, a psychic medium/reader. I'd known her for a long time, and she had shared with me many predictions that had been completely accurate. On this day we were talking about totems, and she looked at me and said I was a white owl. But still, I wasn't sure this was correct. So I waited for a sign to confirm what she'd said. And while I waited, I continued my meditation and prayers that my totem animal would be revealed to me.

Meanwhile, it was the slow season for my business, and so I wasn't ordering any new merchandise. One afternoon I received a phone call from a man who wanted to sell me a kachina for the store.

An authentic kachina is a small wood carving done by a Hopi Indian from the root of a cottonwood tree. It represents one of many deities in the Hopi culture, such as a spirit or a representation of something in the real world. Although kachinas are not worshipped per se, each is viewed as a powerful entity that can, if it is shown the proper respect, use its power for good, bringing, for example, rain, healing, or fertility. For instance, the spirit of the Kokopeli kachina can bring fertility.

The man on the phone who had the Kachina to sell said his name was Lightfoot.. I immediately said that it was my slow season, and that I was not interested in buying any new merchandise. He told me he was a Hopi kachina carver, and he wanted to bring me this kachina he had completed. Again I said, "Thanks, but no. I'm not interested in purchasing any merchandise at this time." He ignored my refusal and insisted that he was supposed to bring this kachina to me.

By now I was annoyed because I'd just told him twice that I wasn't buying anything, let alone a kachina, until business picked up. But he was so insistent that I finally asked him to come to the shop in three or four weeks and I'd buy a few kachinas from him.

The very next morning as I opened the shop, a young Native American appeared holding a kachina. He introduced himself as Lightfoot. We went inside and he set the kachina down carefully on the glass top of the pipe display case. He again began to tell me that he was supposed to bring this kachina to me. Now I was really annoyed, and I thought to myself as I glanced at the kachina, "This guy just won't take no for an answer." I took his information and told him I'd call in three or four weeks and that I needed to get to work. He looked a little confused, but he quietly picked up the kachina and left.

That evening as I meditated, I remembered Lightfoot and his kachina, and it struck me! That kachina, the one I'd barely looked at? It was an image of a white owl, wasn't it? I jumped up and immediately called Lightfoot's number. When he answered, I asked him, "What was that kachina, and what did it represent?'

He answered, "It is the White Snow Owl kachina. It represents intelligence and wisdom. I was instructed to bring it to you."

I was overwhelmed! I felt awful about how annoyed I'd been, and I apologized to him profusely. I added that I'd been asking for my spirit animal to be revealed to me.

When Lightfoot brought me the kachina the next morning, I told him how grateful I was that he'd made it, and that I'd personally take good care of it.

Over the next few months whenever I doubted that this was truly my new totem, somewhere in my surroundings I would see an owl looming closely. Sometime later, a friend asked me to look up from my office chair at the wooden beam that had been directly above my head for the past seven years. It was naturally shaped in the image of an owl. And just weeks after that, when I completed a weekend workshop as I was saying goodbye, I noticed a barn owl perched right above where I was sitting.

I was so excited during the encounter with Lightfoot that I never did get a chance to ask who had instructed him to make this kachina and bring it to me. Nevertheless, I was thankful that my totem had finally been revealed.

CHAPTER 8

Being in Communion

The most valuable possession you can own is an open heart.
~ *Carlos Santana*

Outside my cigar shop was a nice public patio with seating, a water fountain that flowed into a small pond, a three-foot sculpture of Merlin's chair by John Soderberg, and a stage where musicians would sometimes play for tourists and others. This area is depicted in the Hollywood movie *Sedona* as a location for healing. This patio got a lot of sunlight during the day, and I'd spent years sitting there and meditating in the sun on days when business was slow.

I loved sitting in the sun, emptying my mind, and feeling the warmth of the sun's rays as they permeated my body. The experience of relaxing in the sun brought back memories of how, as a high-school student, I'd enjoyed going to the hillside near a neighbor's house, lying in the grass beside the edge of a woods, and napping in the sun after school. This was one of my favorite things to do, because each time I would lie there I could feel the warming power of the sun as it renewed my energy, refreshed my body, and released all of the challenges and anxieties of adolescence and high school. It had always felt wonderful!

When business wasn't slow, I had the privilege of helping my customers select their fine cigars, and sometimes I got to listen to their life stories. Some of these were light and funny, while others were heart-wrenching and painful. But the tone of the story never mattered, because I was so glad to share in their experiences.

Indeed, one reason I opened my tobacco shop had to do with wanting a place where people could come and converse and open their hearts. Another reason involved my desire to work with smoke. Prior to coming to Sedona I'd learned of my Cherokee heritage, and I knew smoke had a spiritual significance – it involved more than just satisfying an urge and having a good time. Smoke can envelope a message sent to heaven, and many times while my customers and I were puffing on our cigars I would send up prayers wrapped in those white billows of smoke.

The time spent with others smoking fine cigars was often a healing experience, both for my customers and myself. On some occasions clients would tell me how grateful they were for my shop and for our conversations. One woman said, "Our time together saved my life. I was on the brink of suicide."

It's truly amazing how we can touch another's life if we're willing to open our hearts and just listen. I call this "Being in Communion," and I use the term to refer to a time when two or more people are gathered together with their hearts wide open.

CHAPTER 9

ILLUMINATION (IN THE LIGHT)

Darkness cannot drive out darkness; only light can do that.
~ Dr. Martin Luther King, Jr.

The first time I experienced being in the light was during the summer of 2007.

One day as I meditated on my smoke shop's patio in the warmth of the summer sun, something started to happen. I felt a tingling in my abdomen. Soon the tingling spread throughout my body. Moments later I felt a cramping sensation. But this wasn't a cramping where muscles hardened, locked up, and immobilized me. Instead, it was challenging and fully engaging, as if every cell in my body was being filled with thousands of orgasms.

It was embarrassing to be experiencing such things in public in the middle of the day, so I hurried inside my shop and sank onto the floor behind the cash register with my back against the wall. Meanwhile, the cramping continued, and my body was rhythmically squeezing and releasing, squeezing and releasing. I didn't want to be alone during this strange experience, and so I began sending thoughts telepathically to my very close friend (who eventually became my lover), Sarah, asking her to come and be with me. Almost immediately she appeared. She entered the shop and was surprised to see me there on the floor behind my cash register. As she came by my side I blurted out, "Lock the doors," and then I asked her to help me to the walk-in cigar humidor. Those were the last words I was able to utter for the next couple of hours. Sarah was a bit fearful about what was going on, but all I could do was lie on the floor for the next two hours as the ecstasy continued.

I knelt on the tile floor with my hands extended in front of me, knees bent and forehead on the floor, as if I were a Muslim recognizing Mecca in the East. I still can remember the cool feeling of the ceramic tile. As energy surged through my body, I felt as if I were praying in some strange way, and I sensed that the feeling was linked to memories of another lifetime.

Meanwhile, I was no longer in control of my body. I was shaking and sweating profusely. All of the sensations I was experiencing were fortunately relieved by moments of relaxation that allowed my body to loosen up briefly. Then the orgasmic shaking and cramping would begin again.

Sometime during this experience I had the sense of entering a bright white diffused light. Its brightness and warmth were dazzling as it filled and surrounded my body, fully consuming me. In addition, the light within my third eye, in the center of my forehead, became so intense that I couldn't distinguish it from myself; there was no sense of separation.

As I entered the light and it entered me, I felt a presence that was beautiful and full of both gentleness and power. Eventually as the light filled my body and my soul, it formed into the shape or silhouette of a hand extended to me. I sensed the presence of potent energy reaching out to me, and inside my head I could hear the words: "It's okay to come." My feeling of being anxious and overwhelmed by the experience then melted into ecstasy and joy, and I was filled with love.

The cramping began to slow, and I gradually returned to the awareness of my physical body. My breath deepened as my lungs became full. I opened my eyes and the first things I saw were all the boxes of cigars – some five hundred of them – that surrounded me there in the walk-in humidor. I still had a feeling that time didn't exist, and as I saw the cigars, I had a deep sense of all the men and women who had ever touched or otherwise helped to create them. I also had a sense of my life flashing before my eyes, but not in a literal way, for I was still beyond time and space: I was given a glimpse of all the events of my life and of how everything fit together. There was a sudden clarity within me that I had never before known.

Trembling and exhausted, I rose to my knees and turned to face Sarah, who was still there with me. She was wearing a Native American -style black velvet blouse and a denim skirt with a Navajo concho belt. As I looked at her, my mind flashed back to one of the many lifetimes we'd spent together. I knew who she was as she sat before me Indian -style with her arms raised toward me. With great love, she was holding me and the energy within me. As I gazed upon her, I heard a voice inside me say, "Don't become attached to her. She, too, has things to do. Just love her."

With Sarah's help, I slowly rose to my feet. I was quite wobbly at first, but I felt in a state of ecstatic bliss. The bliss washed over me in waves, and it was so pervasive that all I could do was smile. I could feel myself smile as if I were the personification of love and compassion. I still couldn't speak, but I didn't need to. With help from another friend, Nadia, Sarah took me to my home. They thought I was still acting strangely – I was still in a state of bliss – and they wanted to make sure I got home safely.

When we got to my place, they both sat on my couch laughing with me as I continued to smile at them with the essence of love that seemed to fill every part of me. We sat there together for a long time, and whenever our eyes met, we filled the room with laughter. I remember feeling that if I were to leave my physical body for any reason, I'd return home to the light.

And all would be well.

CHAPTER 10

Aftermath of Bliss

Do not conform to the pattern of this world, but be transformed by the
renewing of your mind. Then you will be able to test and approve what
God's will is — his good, pleasing and perfect will.
  ~ Romans 12:2

"I live in this world but I am not of it."
  That was the main thought in my mind in the aftermath of being
in the light.

My feelings of bliss lasted for several days, but I gradually returned
to my normal state of awareness. Over the next week or so I had a few
more ecstatic experiences with my body shaking uncontrollably, and
each time Sarah came to my assistance as though our minds were one.

Although I was profoundly moved to have had the experience, I
was confused by it.

Why had it happened?

What did it mean?

What message was I expected to glean from it?

I found several sources that gave some clarity about what had happened to me. But I didn't really know the answers to these questions and
other questions until I was given a book called *Mojud: The Man with the*
Inexplicable Life, containing an ancient Sufi story and a commentary by
Osho (Bhagwan Shree Rajneesh). The book gave me a confirmation that
what had happened was the beginning of a new and beautiful journey.

As Osho says in the book:

> When you go deep into meditation it will happen again and again. A moment will come when your circumference and center are very close, and there is no barrier between them – not even a curtain – and you will hear the center loudly, clearly.

This was what happened to me when I went into the light: my circumference and my center had no barrier between them.

Osho continues:

> Old habits, thoughts will come in, jam your innerways, and the center and the circumference will fall apart. It will happen many times . . . those who are around me – it is going to happen many times. . . . You will come so close to the center that you will feel almost enlightened. You will feel you have arrived, and again it is lost; it's natural.

This was what I experienced in the aftermath of my bliss. After being in the light, after being "so close to the center" that I had felt "almost enlightened," I returned to normal.

Osho also says in the book:

> Suddenly the door opens and you see the vision and there is a lightning experience, and again it is gone and darkness settles.

The doorway to wisdom had indeed opened for me. And now I knew that I was in this world but not of it.

CHAPTER 11

DISMANTLING AND NON-ATTACHMENT

Even though I walk through the valley of the shadow of death, I will fear
no evil, for you are with me; your rod and your staff, they comfort me.
~ Psalm 23:4

I lost everything.

After my experience of being in the light, the weeks and months passed. And as they did, all the things for which I had worked so hard for so many years – my business of eleven years, my home, my truck – one by one, I lost them.

My world seemed to be imploding right in front of me. And there was nothing I could do but to surrender.

Surrender my life as I knew it.

My long-time friends were puzzled by my inability to make even the simplest decisions. Up to this point, making decisions had always been easy for me. I had worked since I was a seven-year-old boy delivering newspapers, and had risen to a corporate job of managing and administering millions of dollars of retirement plans. One friend (a real-estate investor with numerous properties in Texas) said I was in what he called a "purple haze"; he said I could no longer find the balance of being in the world. Another friend (who lived in Chicago with a wife, two boys, three mortgages, and challenges of his own) tried to give me advice about living a life I wanted to let go of. They both meant well, and on many occasions their words were like life rafts to me, but now, they couldn't help me. I was, it seemed, beyond help.

Daniel, another friend for fourteen years, didn't give unsolicited advice. He just listened and gave me affirmations for where I was and what I was learning. He always called at a time when I needed to be heard and not advised. I appreciated my other friends, of course, but Daniel's way of interacting with me was what I needed at the time.

And then there was Grandfather Morning Owl, my friend, father, and grandfather all wrapped into one. Our friendship and his wisdom and teachings would make up a book unto itself.

Over the next two years I struggled to understand the world that surrounded me. And in so doing, I was in a constant state of confusion. "Why am I here?" I would ask. Nothing made sense. The material world – its people and things – just didn't matter. Each day I would struggle to get out of bed. The immensity of life weighed heavily on me.

And my brain felt so much physical pain that it seemed to be a separate entity and not part of my body. There was a constant high-pitched buzzing in my head, and the feeling of a tight and constricting stocking cap on my scalp. It was all just too much at times. I didn't even know how to describe what I was feeling. The best I could do would be to say that all the synapses in my brain were cross-firing, or misfiring. Nothing was at peace or at rest inside my head.

I fell into a state of depression that was so deep that I wasn't sure if I'd be on the planet much longer. I just couldn't seem to go back to my old ways of being and of understanding life. The ends of my fingers were peeling away, leaving them raw and sore, something I'd experienced seventeen years before during my corporate job in Chicago. For days and weeks my body would be a raw bundle of nerves. I struggled with the thought that I was going mad. I clung to a sense of hope as I dangled from the cliff of existence. But at times, I just wanted to die.

I even pleaded with God to take my life so I wouldn't suffer any longer.

The pain was just too great.

CHAPTER 12

Insanity?

A man who is "of sound mind" is one who keeps the inner madman under lock and key.
    ~ *Paul Valery*

I thought I was going insane.
And I was terrified.
I was scared that any minute I might be in a straightjacket and hauled off to a psych ward.

I begged God and all the angels, archangels, saints, Buddha, spirits, gods, and goddesses to please, please help me.

My well-meaning friends, in their attempts to comfort me, gave advice that seemed trivial and superficial; things like, "Just breathe through it and you'll be okay." But I wasn't okay, and their words landed on deaf ears.

My friend Sarah had been encouraging me to get professional help, and eventually, I agreed. I tested the waters by talking with a friend of hers, a psychotherapist in Rochester, New York. That conversation went okay, so I found a psychiatrist and spent an hour revealing my family history and my current plight. His response was quick and precise: "You have post-traumatic stress disorder," he said, and wrote a prescription for an antidepressant.

I was very reluctant to add drugs to my situation. I knew that anti-depressants were popular medications used by and helpful to millions of people. But I also know they had side effects that included suicide and mental symptoms that were worse than what I already had. My mother had experienced deep depression and near suicide, and a sibling had been hospitalized committed for a mental breakdown. This family history made the idea of taking drugs nearly unbearable to me. But I knew I had to do something. So I decided to take the drugs.

For a week I took the drug and gradually increased the dosage as per the doctor's instructions. (I later learned that the dosage was mild compared to what was normally prescribed.) Within seven days, however, my emotional and physical body felt numb. That Sunday as I listened to a sermon, I noticed I had no emotional response to anything being said. This was the worst feeling yet; I'd rather die than be numb to the world. My emotional sensitivity was one of the traits that I valued most about myself, and I didn't want to let go of it. So I stopped taking the medication and decided to put myself into God's hands.

Without the medication, I went back to my depression and my desire to die. And my spiritual contact with God was nowhere to be found. I was in hell.

On a few occasions I considered taking my revolver out of the closet and ending the excruciating pain I felt. But as bad as things were, suicide was never really an option. Something inside of me wanted to live rather than to end my existence on earth. So I kept going as best I could, and each second seemed to contain an eternity.

As I continued to struggle physically, spiritually, and emotionally, several friends continued to provide support. These included my teacher Grandfather Morning Owl, a friend named Kyle, and my brother Keith. My friendship with Jacob, a guy from Chicago that I'd known for twenty years, was a comfort to me because it gave me a sense of history. Another friend, a woman whom I'd known for ten years, offered me a small, comfortable studio in exchange for doing some work on the property. I was fortunate to have these friends and their love.

Meanwhile, Sarah looked for and found a number of books that she thought might help me; I read them, but nothing worked. Nevertheless, Sarah was the most important person in my life at this time.

I had come to believe that we'd shared past lives and that we'd made an agreement to come together again in this life as well. Our love seemed to persist through my issues with abandonment to my troubles with finances, and our feelings were so deep and profound that I'm not sure I'll ever experience such depth again.

I moved into the small studio, which my friends called "the monastic chamber." I soon learned that Kenny Loggins was going to rent the main house. Kenny's music in general and one song in particular – "Celebrate Me Home" – spoke to my soul. The words comforted me with the assurance that my home was in the light, the light that I'd gone into months before. Kenny and I crossed paths several times in Sedona, but always only briefly. I wanted to give him his privacy.

CHAPTER 13

SERVICE

Take time first to be holy. Don't let a day go by without meditation and prayer for some definite purpose, and not for self, but that self may be the channel of help to someone else. For in helping others is the greater way to help self.

    ~ *Edgar Cayce*

The clairvoyant and psychic healer Edgar Cayce said that being of service to others is a way to combat depression, and this was true for me. Indeed, being of service was one of the very few things that helped me. The woman who owned the little studio, my "monastic chamber," belonged to Saint Andrews Episcopal Church in West Sedona, and this church sponsored meals for the needy. I volunteered there every Monday evening, preparing or serving food, or washing dishes afterward. I always felt much better when I did this humanitarian work.

For months Sarah and others around me had been telling me that I had a gift as a teacher who could help others with spiritual healing. I twice heard a voice telling me to go to the Unity Village and Campus in Missouri. Located in a suburb of Kansas City, this is the world headquarters of the Unity Church. I was told to go there to seek training to become a minister.

I responded the first time by actually going to Unity Village in Missouri. During this first visit I was approached by an older woman who asked me if I was a minister. Without thinking, I responded, "No. Not yet." I later learned that her name was Mrs. Appleton. She was with the Unity Institute and Seminary and could always predict with great accuracy who would be called to the ministry.

The second time I was awakened by a voice that sounded exactly like that of Mrs. Appleton herself. The voice told me to return to Unity Village. So I flew back to Missouri. As I pulled up to the campus, I was talking on my cell phone with Sarah, and she had just told me to be open to the divine inside me and to accept my gifts.

As I arrived at Unity Village, a church service was going on. I went inside the church and sat down; as I did, something happened deep inside of me. My tears began to flow right there in the middle of the church service. Sobbing and gasping for air, I clutched my heart with both of my arms firmly locked around me. I tried to control my emotions because I didn't want to disturb the church service and all of the people sitting around me. Meanwhile, I was so overcome with emotion that I was oblivious to what the minister was saying.

Inside my head, a voice was telling me, "Get up and go down to the stage." But I resisted this command. I wasn't ready.

After the service I regained my composure, and in the greeting area of the church, I asked the minister, "What did you speak about?"

He responded by pointing to a place in the church where CDs were sold, and he said, "You can purchase the CD of the morning service over there."

I bought the newly recorded CD and went out to my car and popped it into the player. The words on the CD were just what Sarah and others had been telling me all along. The message was that each of us should accept our gifts and be present in the world. I grabbed my cell phone to tell Sarah what had happened and what the message was on the CD. And of course, her response was: "See! I've been telling you that all along."

I regretted not having gone to the front of the church during the service that day, but life had other lessons in store for me. I returned to Sedona and continued to attend Unity Spiritual Center. One day at church a man told a story about how he had gone to Unity at the exact time I was there. His experiences were nearly identical to mine.

77

But he had followed the divine directive and I hadn't. This caused me to feel disappointment in myself, because I hadn't stepped up to the plate to do my required spiritual work. But as time went on, I watched this man's connection with the church fall into disruption and chaos. This was a sign to me that perhaps I wasn't ready, after all, and so I better accepted myself for being where I was at the time.

CHAPTER 14

Finding My Home

Make a home for yourself inside your own head. You'll find what you need
to furnish it – memory, friends you can trust, love of learning, and other
such things. That way it will go with you wherever you journey.
  ~ Tad Williams

Bit by bit, the deep depression and mood swings began to be replaced with learning, awareness, and meaning. One of the more powerful books that I read at about this time was called *Spiritual Emergency.* The book gave me some peace and understanding about what was going on in my body.

Another book I read was about kundalini. Kundalini is a word for the body's life force or energy. I learned about the effects of kundalini and its power as it moves up and down the spine. I came to the conclusion that our bodies are miraculous gifts.

My teacher Grandfather Morning Owl had said to me many times, "Don't try to take heaven by storm." I began to comprehend the magnitude of that statement. I also came to understand that Jesus experienced a special kind of energy and a knowledge of the divine, just as Buddha, Krishna, and others had experienced, and that these men were our guides, showing us the path within spiritually so that we might attain enlightenment by recognizing that they and we and God are one. To some religions these ideas might be blasphemous, but this is the truth as I understand it today. Jesus was a man, and the

"Light of Christ" was the light of God being experienced through him.

My way of responding to the call to the ministry was to enroll at the University of Santa Monica to pursue a master's degree in spiritual psychology. While I was there, I read some essays by an Italian psychologist named Roberto Assagioli. Assagioli is perhaps best known for developing the science of psychosynthesis, a spiritual approach to psychology; indeed, he was one of the first to integrate the concept of spirituality with the field of psychology.

Reading Assagioli's essays helped me understand what I had gone through, because he described the effects of too much kundalini energy in one's body: it can even take away your life if you're not ready to assimilate its effects. Assagioli described very accurately what had happened to me.

Assagioli's essays gave me a tremendous sense of relief. Here was someone who fully described and understood my experiences. I felt as if a heavy weight had been lifted from my shoulders. I was also relieved to know that I wasn't going crazy. (During my master's program studies, I became friends with a woman who had been committed to a psychiatric ward and medicated for having similar experiences.) Now, having read Assagioli, I felt I was beginning to get a grip on life. Step by step I was coming back to the world and to my body.

Once again, the admonition not to try to take heaven by storm came through loud and clear. Meanwhile I became aware that I needed to be careful about asking for new experiences. Now I ask that each new experience be filled with ease and grace.

However, I continued to struggle with the meaning of life and with the question of "Why did I have these experiences?" As I sought to solve this problem, one answer in particular stood out: I had been shown a place that I call home, a place we all came from, a place beyond this physical plane of earth. Ultimately, my experiences have invited me to be more present and more loving in the earthly world, and to ultimately see the beauty that is all around us. I'm still learning to be present in each moment and in the "now" of life. I also now understand that we are all in this life together, and that not one of us will be left behind in the process of awakening.

I recently came across this quote from the inspirational writer, Courtney A. Walsh, that perhaps helps illustrate what I'm talking about:

> Dear Human: You've got it all wrong. You didn't come here to master unconditional love. That is where you came from and where you'll return. You came here to learn personal love. Universal love. Messy love. Sweaty love. Crazy love. Broken love. Whole love. Infused with divinity. Lived through the grace of stumbling. Demonstrated through the beauty of . . . messing up. Often. You didn't come here to be perfect. You already are. You came here to be gorgeously human. Flawed and fabulous. And then to rise again into remembering.

Meanwhile, as time went on, I began to see my experiences in a different light: they were lessons to me about being more present in my life and about valuing each moment to appreciate all of life's beauty.

Of course, I still have struggles – emotional highs and lows – and I'm learning to see these, too, as lessons. Usually when I have enough distance from a bad situation I can see that the cloud has a silver lining. As I continue to learn patience, and to get out of my own way, I can see the synchronicities all around me and surrender to the flow of my life, extracting the silver linings. This is when life itself becomes the meditation.

Understanding my emotional triggers previously took months if not years; today it takes only days and sometimes even mere moments. It is this healing that continually deepens and gives me life. Each new experience, whether good or bad, brings with it the knowledge that where I am is perfect and that I will be just fine.

CHAPTER 15

The Feminine

The woman's mission is not to enhance the masculine spirit, but to express the feminine; hers is not to preserve a man-made world, but to create a human world by the infusion of the feminine element into all of its activities.
~ Margaret Thatcher

Sigmund Freud once said, "The great question that has never been answered, and which I have not yet been able to answer, despite my thirty years of research into the feminine soul, is 'What does a woman want?'"

I might be wrong about this, but I believe that what most women really want is someone to talk with them as equals, to share with them from a heart-felt place and to really listen to what they are saying. Doing this has always come fairly easily to me.

One of the things I've realized about men in our Western culture is our inability to describe what we are feeling. You would think it would be so simple, wouldn't you? But instead of knowing their feelings, men have historically been providers. Our society has been based on men being doers, being competitive, and distrusting one another.

Women, on the other hand, seem to express their feelings easily, especially with other women. Women have historically been caretakers who bring new life into the world. As a result, as a teacher of mine says, while men tend to make and execute decisions autonomously, women more easily make decisions collectively – through a consortium.

Eastern thought differentiates between male and female energy, or yin and yang. The yin or feminine is thought of as slow, soft, and yielding; the yang is fast, hard, and solid. So feminine energy is gentle, receptive, and open and is comfortable with being vulnerable. It isn't concerned so much with doing but with being heard and felt. Masculine energy is one of doing and of completion – it's an energy that wants to get things done, and it can be aggressive at times as well.

I believe that each man and each woman contains both feminine and masculine energies. Both of these energies have a place within each individual's being and psyche. Neither is more important than the other. One's ability to flow between each of these energies is based on what is needed in the given situation. But they are rarely seen in balance within a single individual.

I've been told that I have a better balance than most of these two energies, and this is surprising, given my upbringing. As I mentioned earlier, my parents – especially my mother – were mostly absent during a critical point in my life. They'd been busy caring for my brother Ken, who eventually died of leukemia when I was seven. My older brother and sister have many stories about how loving and happy our mother was before the death of her son, our brother. But after that, and at a critical point in my own development, she was challenged mentally and psychiatrically. I did have some experiences with her that were loving and nurturing – but not many. Over the years, I've come to a place of forgiveness for my mother. I've struggled to reframe my perceptions of her, and I have begun to recognize her beauty.

In spite of the absence of my mother from my life as I grew up, from an early age I seemed to have a knack of easily relating to and talking with females. In my teens and early twenties, when my friends were off in search of sex, or alcohol, or both, I enjoyed just sitting with my girlfriend and talking about life and spiritual things.

Meanwhile, my buddies would say things like, "Man, you always get the chicks." What they didn't understand was that what the "chicks" wanted was just to be listened to as equals, and this was something that for some reason I was easily able to do – and something I enjoyed doing, as well. So my friends thought I had an easy time attracting women, and maybe I did, but this was because I wasn't like the other guys who wanted to just have their way with women and then brag about it. I was more interested in an emotional connection with a female before I would be with her intimately and sexually.

Meanwhile, the attention I got from the females was great, but at times I felt my mindset was almost a curse that I couldn't separate myself from. My supposed ease in attracting women led to more than a few problems with the guys. Boyfriends sometimes suggested that I was flirting with or even sleeping with their girlfriends. On at least one occasion, this led to a punch and a bloody lip! But in the end, it didn't matter what the guys thought, because I was who I was and it felt right.

Meanwhile, some of my girlfriends, too, would become pretty jealous because I related so well to women other than themselves. I would try to console them, but my efforts usually fell short. Even my last girlfriend, Sarah, with whom I had a beautiful relationship, felt threatened by my friendships with other women on several occasions.

Nevertheless, I'm grateful for my understanding and appreciation of women. I grew up with three sisters whom I adore. It wasn't until my early adult life that I became close to my other brother who became a priest.

So I have come to understand that all human beings have masculine and feminine energies. But before I really understood this, I wanted to know more about what the feminine aspect was like. It was only a year ago that something happened that gave me a glimpse into what I had asked for.

While I was in California in graduate school studying for my master's degree in spiritual psychology, a classmate sent out a video in which men were apologizing. They apologized to the women they were with, ones that they had hurt in some way, and they apologized to women in general, for being patriarchal throughout history and for the trauma that men had visited upon women over many lifetimes and generations.

When I saw the video on YouTube I felt and appreciated the sincerity of the apologies – but something about it didn't sit right with me. For example, I felt that men, too, had been harmed physically, mentally, and verbally. Something seemed to be missing in the whole equation. I prayed to God to reveal the deeper meaning of the video.

My uneasiness even played out with my girlfriend Sarah. Her predominant character was of masculine energies, of getting things done. Over the years I had found this to be both helpful and agitating. But this video seemed to bring both of our issues to the surface.

During the next couple of weeks after I saw the video, we got into some pretty heated discussions around the apologies. Her argument was that men had, over the centuries, been very destructive. I agreed, but I felt that men had suffered, too. Somehow we let the issue alone for several days, and deep within I knew that both of us were right. But in those moments when each of us wanted to be heard, our own opinions seemed to be the most important.

I was reading a book by the British Sufi mystic Llewellyn Vaughan-Lee called *The Face before I Was Born*. It was his spiritual autobiography. Just as I was coming to the end of the book, I began to sense that something was happening inside of me. I knew on one hand that Sarah was in the truth, but at the same time I knew that what I felt was also true.

One night as I reached the end of the book I had a dream. The dream revealed to me that the pain of our disagreement on this issue went beyond each of our own stories, and that something else needed to be healed. It was something deep inside of me, and something that affected all of creation, Mother Earth, and every one of us. It went back to the time of creation or what some call the Garden of Eden.

I awoke feeling about to explode – but not in a bad way. I had the sense that something was going to open up, as though I'd reached a boundary with the truth on the other side. I was alone that morning, as my girlfriend was sleeping in, so I brewed some tea, sat down on the couch, and opened the book *The Face before I Was Born*. As I read, my inner dimension, my soul, seemed to open to a space greater than what I understood at that moment. Here is a sampling of the words:

> All inner work requires a feminine attitude, of nurturing and letting go. . . . Individuals . . . had become conditioned by a masculine culture that says you must improve yourself, struggle to be other than what you are.

The author went on to talk about travel into the archetypal world and how he entered that world with others. And then he continued:

> The archetypes need to talk to us. For so long they have been locked deep in the unconscious and many people only experience them through phobias. . . . Often the first figure we encountered was the wounded feminine, who cannot see through her tears. The depth of her pain was a powerful reminder that our masculine culture has caused a deep inner wound. . . . Not only have we cut ourselves off from our inner psychic foundations, but the archetypes themselves have become wounded and sorrowful through isolation and neglect.

I suddenly realized this was what my dream had been about. And I remembered asking God to reveal to me the deeper meaning about the video. Within seconds of finishing the words reprinted above, I felt as if a veil had been removed from between my innermost depths and the circumference of my being. As these two parts of myself began to converge, I felt a deep pain – the pain that Llewellyn Vaughan-Lee had described as "the wounded feminine."

I realized the pain I was feeling was what all the women in the world had felt at one time or another. My tears flowed, and I gasped for air. And then my awareness and emotions transformed and focused on Mother Earth and all of the pain we have caused her. Suddenly my body was a vacuum that sucked all of these understandings back into me (or opened me to them), and I realized that I was connecting to the feminine aspect of myself. A place of openness and receptivity emerged and opened me up.

As I lay on the couch, I felt deep sadness and joy simultaneously. The sadness was that some part of me had once been gone from my psyche; it had now returned, I had remembered it again, or it was reflected back to me. The joy was the joy of feminine energy. These seeming opposites of pain and joy held the same space within me (I call it the dynamic tension of my soul), and I felt transformed.

I now understood what I had asked for, and that was to comprehend very deeply what the video represented to me and to the feminine aspect of myself.

My heart space expanded, filling the room, and I was able to grasp the ancient knowledge of the archetype that Llewellyn Vaughan-Lee had described. It had opened a doorway for me to enter this profound experience.

Afterward, I came to know what the men in the video were trying to share with the women of the world. It was the same thing that I was now trying to say and experience. It wasn't just forgiveness that they were asking for; it was, ultimately, for the feminine archetype within themselves and all of creation to be at peace. And for the feminine to be remembered, honored, integrated, and healed. (I believe that as we heal, we experience the return to wholeness of an aspect of our soul that has been separated from our essence.) In that moment I was remembering my connection and my oneness with the feminine-and ultimately with the one divine source that we call God.

CHAPTER 16

A BROTHER'S LOVE

There's no other love like the love for a brother. There's no other love like the love from a brother.
~ Terri Guillemets

It was like a sci-fi movie where an alien tears itself from a human's body. I experienced a deep healing, but with it came a substantial amount of pain.

I'd been working in Sedona at an auto body repair facility as an estimator. On weekends, Sarah and I were traveling to Los Angeles for weekend graduate school courses. Classes began at 6:45 p.m. and lasted until 10:45 p.m. on Friday nights. Saturday and Sunday classes were from 9 a.m. until 11:00 p.m. Because I was studying spiritual psychology, we were working with the emotions. Each class was intense.

One evening after class my girlfriend Sarah and I headed out to the Whole Foods store on Wilshire Avenue in Santa Monica. Class that evening had been even more powerful than usual, and now lots of feelings were bubbling up to the surface. I didn't want to experience these emotions at all, especially not in the parking lot of a grocery store. But I had to begin to surrender to emotional experiences and to release my own sense of control. I realized that I'd have to embrace these emotions to release them.

I took a deep breath, and suddenly I was paralyzed. I mean

literally. I couldn't lift my arms. Sensing what was happening, Sarah encouraged me to love that part of me that was in turmoil and to allow it to come forward. I was still frozen and couldn't respond, but I knew she was right.

We sat a bit longer in the parking lot. I continued breathing deeply, and I began to feel a bit less immobilized. By now it was nearly midnight, and Sarah finally asked if I was able to drive. I checked in with myself, and then said, "Yes. I can drive." When we arrived back at our hotel, I collapsed on the bed and fell into a fitful sleep, tossing and turning all night.

The emotional and physical discomfort ebbed and flowed throughout the weekend. During that time, I noticed that a lot of frustration and anger was building up inside me. On Sunday, just as we boarded the plane to go back to Arizona, all of the physical and emotional symptoms began coming again with full force. I took my seat on the aisle thinking, "Oh God, not now!" As the plane taxied down the runway, I could barely contain my feelings of anger and frustration and sadness. I knew I had to be alone, so I told Sarah I was moving to another seat to deal with was going on by myself.

This was a new response for me. In the past, when I would be flooded with emotions, I'd often unleash them onto those closest to me. But now I was conscious of the deep hurt I would cause if I allowed this to happen. So I moved up several aisles and sat by the window, away from the other passengers on the plane.

Free-form writing was a technique that I'd learned about for people dealing with intense emotions. So I pulled a notebook and a pen from my backpack, and I began to write. Soon I was scribbling with such intensity that the pen was tearing the pages. I began to write, "What the hell is going on?" as strange feelings of anger seethed inside me. Again and again I wrote those words: "What the hell is going on?"

Suddenly thoughts of my older brother Ken, who had died of leukemia at the age of twelve, filled my mind. It was as if he were a guardian spirit that I could communicate with. As the plane soared gently through the air, I mentally pleaded with him to help me get through this, and for him to reveal what these feelings were about.

When I was a young boy Ken, as my older brother, had saved me from many conflicts. He'd always seemed to show up whenever I was in need. Now I found myself thinking about how, when he died, I hadn't been allowed to see him or to be included in anything having to do with his funeral and burial. I'd never had the chance to say goodbye to him; instead, he'd just disappeared from my life.

As these thoughts filled my mind, my anger turned to sadness. I thought of how, over the course of my life, so many people have said, "Kevin, you live with one foot in this world and one foot in the spirit world." Now I was understanding why.

I found myself pleading asking, "Ken, why haven't you let me go?"

And then I heard the words from him: "Why haven't *you* let go of *me*, Kevin?"

In that moment, everything stood still. He was right. I hadn't let go of him. I took a deep breath in spite of my tears, and I realized that was the truth that had caused my near-breakdown and paralysis two evenings earlier in the Whole Foods parking lot. And perhaps many other times, as well.

After hearing those words from my brother – "Why haven't *you* let go of *me*, Kevin?" – the anger and frustration I was feeling subsided. These were replaced with a deep sense of peace and calm that I have experienced only a few times in my life.

Looking back on this experience now, I realize that healing comes in waves and progressions, and that it was my responsibility to allow it to happen. But I had needed to be open to my feelings and to the physical signs that my body brought forth. And when the right time came, I had to get out of my own way.

Now, as the plane continued its flight toward Phoenix, I took another deep breath and recognized that the pain I'd felt all weekend was gone. My mind was quiet and my body was at peace. Not only that, but I had an awareness of intense compassion and love for my brother and for myself, along with a strong sense of closure.

Deep inside my mind I held both of us, my brother and myself, in love and compassion for the rest of the flight home.

CHAPTER 17

The Compound

The only power that exists is inside ourselves.
~ Anne Rice, Interview with the Vampire

Dracula. Frankenstein. The Werewolf. Those movies are just fiction, right? I used to think so. But based on an experience I had in 2010, I'm no longer sure.

Sedona is gorgeous in any season, but that fall it was perhaps a bit less beautiful. It was colder than usual. The crimson and gold leaves had fallen early from the cottonwood and sycamore trees and the red oaks along Oak Creek. The sky was often overcast and grey.

Meanwhile, I was busy helping launch a new company in the fitness industry. My colleague in this project was brilliant; but he had a tyrannical side. Nevertheless, when he invited Sarah and me on a trip to Europe, of course we accepted.

We were to visit a place in Europe where we would meet up with his colleague. This sounded innocent enough at the time, but after what happened, thinking about it today makes my blood run cold; therefore, I'm reluctant to name the small town or even the country for fear of causing a resurgence of the negative energy that I experienced there. Suffice it to say that it was a community with a reputation as a modern marvel for its eco-driven technology and its breakthroughs in healing. The psychology professor there had dedicated his life to developing new ways of healing the body and the spirit.

Sarah had been to this particular part of Europe before, and I was looking forward to experiencing it with her. So we packed our bags and headed for Sky Harbor Airport in Phoenix. Although the trip was fourteen hours long, we had a terrific flight because Sarah had sprung for first-class upgrades. We lounged in our oversized seats, covered ourselves in our warm cozy blankets, and fell soundly asleep for most of the flight. In the capital, we transferred to a train, and watched the European countryside pass by the windows as we zipped along toward our destination.

We'd already experienced several delays along the way, but it wasn't until we arrived in the small town that things got challenging. No one spoke English, and we couldn't speak the local language. We were there to spend a week at the eco-driven community, but we needed to get there by cab and there were no cabs in sight. I tried without success to explain what we wanted to the folks at the small train station, but no one understood me. Finally a cab showed up. We got in and after a half-hour ride deeper into the countryside, we pulled up to a compound with a high wall around it and iron gates at the entrance. There was an admissions building, and the cab driver took us there. We had arrived hours later than expected due to all the delays, and so there was some confusion about who we were and where we were to stay. I had begun to wonder about what was going on. This was supposedly a world-renowned community, but the people at the local train station seemed to know nothing about it. And why was an eco-driven community housed in a compound?

I put these thoughts out of my mind when we finally connected with the admissions coordinator, who gave us our keys and directed us to a second-floor room at the end of the hallway. There was nothing remarkable about the room. It was very simply furnished, with two double beds. Exhausted from our travels, we had a good night's sleep.

The following morning we met up with my colleague and his wife. They took us around and introduced us. As we toured the labyrinth of buildings, we were treated with great respect by everyone at the compound as a result of my colleague's credentials, and because the four of us were to be trained in the healing modalities the professor had developed so we could bring these techniques back to the United States.

As we learned about the philosophies and the research of the people at the compound, we were quite impressed. One thing that particularly interested me was their work with plants. One afternoon early in our stay they showed us a plant hooked up to a synthesizer that could emit different sounds and even music. Each of us was asked to walk over to the plant to see what sound it would make. When my girlfriend and I walked within a foot of the plant, the synthesizer emitted a simple and melodious tune. We tried this several more times and each time the response was essentially the same, but when my colleague and his wife approached the plant, the melody was significantly different.

Time and time again I was amazed as we were shown other tests and experiments that the people at the compound were conducting. For example, in one experiment electrodes were hooked up to a plant and to the lock on the front door of a house. When the door opened, the plant could sense if the person at the door was familiar. If so the plant, using the electrodes, would open the door. But if the person at the door was a stranger, someone unfamiliar to the plant, the door would remain locked.

The people at the compound also said that they were teaching the plants a language. My mind was ablaze with possibilities! I thought, "What if the redwoods could talk to us? What a story they could tell!"

I later learned that this kind of plant research was not unique to the compound. Indeed, I later saw a film produced by the son of Danny Thomas and the Saint Jude Children's Research Hospital that showed similar studies with plants. But at the time, all this was new to me. And I was very impressed.

On the second evening of our stay, we were invited to dinner at the professor's home in the countryside along with the founder and several other key people. When we entered the home, we were introduced to everyone. But they seemed quite detached and aloof. This was odd because we were prospective teachers who would bring their healing modalities to the United States. At least that is what they'd said they wanted with us.

We were served an assortment of fresh cheeses and a dinner prepared just for us. But strangely, during the dinner although we were only about eighteen inches away, we were separated from them by a seven-foot-high cloth partition. We were unable to see them.

During dinner I had the strange feeling that they all were from another world. I had stranger feelings when I looked at them. "This is odd," I thought.

Early on the morning of the third day we were shown into a room that we were told was not normally open to outsiders. As soon as the door opened, I wanted out of there right away. The room was filled with copper wires and capacitors that led to an enormous contraption in the center that was constructed, in part, out of large crystals. On a side wall was the outline of a human body surrounded by more copper wires. It looked like something out of a Frankenstein movie.

I asked the administrator, "What is all of this for?" Her response was that it was used to map a person's DNA. When she said that, Sarah and I slowly began to head for the door.

But as we were halfway there, I noticed a number of copper wires going up through the ceiling. I stared, dumbfounded with the realization that our room was just above this one. What was going on?

We graciously excused ourselves and went upstairs to our room. After searching for just a few minutes, we found it in the closet: a copper wire with some kind of a capacitor attached to its end. I took the fingernail clippers from my shaving kit and snipped the wire right where it came out of the wall. Sarah told me not to, but my response was, "I'm not letting them tap into our energy."

Nevertheless, we didn't leave the compound that day. Part of me was still hopeful about the potential of what I'd seen. Part of me believed – or wanted to believe – that what was happening in this community could make the world a better place.

The following morning we were trained in a healing modality that requires touching the body with subtle pressure. During this training session, as we observed the professor demonstrating the movements, tears rolled down my cheeks. This caught the attention of the professor, my colleague and his wife, and the woman lying on the massage table for the demonstration. Not wanting to distract attention from the lesson, I waved my hand to acknowledge that I was okay. But my emotions grew stronger and my heart's energy filled the room.

Suddenly, I felt the presence of my deceased brother, Ken.

The professor was still noticing that something was going on with me, and he asked me to share what was happening. I described it as best I could, saying that my heart was wide open and I felt as though I were seeing into another dimension. Meanwhile, simultaneously I was experiencing sadness, joy, and compassion. I knew the energy engulfing me was about to reveal something. But I didn't have a clue what it would be.

We took a lunch break, and during lunch I could feel my heart continue to open. There was a sense of fullness in my body's energy, and this stayed with me until late that evening. Meanwhile, as we sat at lunch talking with others who were not living there in the compound, I noticed something very unusual: their eyes gleamed with life and with the happiness of sharing their life stories. This was unusual because everyone else I'd met at the compound had seemed almost lifeless. Instead of gleaming, their eyes seemed to stare dully, without expression. I'd seen no emotions displayed: no happiness, no sadness, no expression of any feelings at all. It was if someone had drained the life out of them.

We finished lunch and Sarah and I went to our room. We wanted to rest up, because that evening the founder of the community was going to give an important speech in the auditorium. After our rest and before the presentation, we decided to view a collection of artwork that the people in the compound were very proud of, artwork that had been created by the founder. To us they seemed peculiar, with a use of florescent paints that made them look like something out of the psychedelic sixties. Indeed, there were even black lights to illuminate some of them, revealing a layer of art that was invisible with the naked eye. As I looked at the artworks, I knew something was not right. My heart space was still wide open, the spirit of my deceased brother was still with me, and I knew that these works of art were not of the "Light." They were, instead, of the "Darkness."

The speech was about to begin, so we headed down the long hallway to the auditorium. As Sarah and I walked along the corridor we saw several members of the community walking toward us from the other direction. And as they approached, a scene from a movie entered my consciousness.

It was the film Interview with the Vampire, starring Brad Pitt, Tom Cruise, and Antonio Banderas. In this scene Banderas, who plays the vampire Armand, is standing in a crypt full of vampires. At that moment, there in the hallway, I had the sudden chilling realization that vampires do exist. This knowledge was not from a place of intellect but from deep within my soul. And at that moment I knew this truth beyond a shadow of a doubt.

We continued walking toward the auditorium, and the people who passed us looked at my girlfriend as though she were their prey. But I knew these weren't the blood-sucking breed of vampires from the movie; instead, these were the kind that would take your energy and your soul. As I saw each one size up my girlfriend, I would look directly into his or her eyes, and just as my eyes made the connection, each one would immediately look away. The experience was even more unsettling because as I engaged them eye-to-eye I could literally see through their eyelids. Their eye sockets were deep and black. It was like looking into sheer darkness.

Sarah had been with me during many ecstatic and strange experiences, and she knew in that moment that I was seeing something profound and frightening. Clutching my arm she whispered, "What is going on?" I explained what had just happened and that we needed to get out of the hallway. "Now!" I said. There was an empty room to our left, and we ducked into it. I was still keenly aware of my brother's energy and of my heart's opening. And I felt protected: my heart was a beacon of light from a lighthouse. But still, I feared for Sarah's safety.

For the next several minutes we prayed to be wrapped in divine light and that this light would be sent ahead of us along our path that evening. We also prayed for the light to surround everyone there; we refrained from judging these people because they, too, were an aspect of God.

Minutes later we were interrupted as my colleague and his friend entered the room. He could see I was still experiencing what he'd observed earlier that day. He said that I should go back to my room, and that he'd escort Sarah with him to the lecture. I wasn't about to let that happen. I looked directly at him and said, "We'll be there for the founder's speech, but I need you to leave us alone right now."

I don't remember much about the presentation, probably because I was so focused on planning to leave.

We departed the following morning. As we left, we prayed for the community and everyone there, again feeling that they were all an aspect of God. I had a confidence deep inside that someday they would shift the balance from darkness to light. We held those thoughts in our minds as we loaded our belongings into a cab and took our seats inside.

We each breathed a sigh of relief as the cab rolled through the high wrought-iron front gates, leaving the compound behind forever and moving back into safety.

CHAPTER 18

A FATHER AND SON

I knew my father had done the best he could, and I had no regrets about the way I'd turned out. Regrets about the journey, maybe, but not the destination.

> ~ *Nicholas Sparks*

Someone was knocking on my door, and I was annoyed. I was busy. I was struggling with a paper for my graduate school class, and I didn't want to be disturbed.

The paper was about my father: how I wished he had shown me more love, or at least acknowledged me once and a while. He'd never been affectionate or even supportive toward me. Some of my paper was based on the work of John Bradshaw, the Houston -based counselor and writer who pioneered the idea of the "inner child."

Like me, Bradshaw was born into a dysfunctional family; indeed, he was the one who brought the term "dysfunctional family" into American consciousness. Also like me, he'd been emotionally abandoned by his father, and he became a high achiever. Like my older brother who became a priest, Bradshaw studied for the priesthood. His books and his approach to therapy involve getting in touch with memories of distressing childhood experiences, and with how one's wounded or neglected inner child might be causing pain.

This was what I was trying to do as I worked on my grad school paper. I was hurt that my father had chosen not to be there for me. Feelings of being alone and abandoned were rising up in me, bringing tears to my eyes. I was using every technique I knew of to deal with them – deep breathing, self-affirmations, positive mantras, and so on – but nothing seemed to help. I was so upset by my thoughts about my father, about how his aloofness had driven me to a lifelong sense of abandonment and loss, that I couldn't even write.

I had to get the paper written, so I asked God for an experience that might provide a sense of love coming to me from my father and resolve these issues so I could get back to work on the assignment. With this request in mind, I heard the disruptive knock at the door.

I thought, "Who the heck is knocking on my door this early afternoon? Don't they know I'm busy writing and don't want to be disturbed?" People never knock on my door unless they are coming to visit me, and I nearly always know about the visit in advance.

The knocking continued. Whoever was there wasn't going away. So I wiped the tears from my eyes, took another deep breath, and headed for the front door. Not knowing who it was, I cracked the door open just a little bit, and there stood a young boy around the age of eight or nine.

Standing close behind him was a man who had his hand lightly touching the boy on his shoulder. They appeared to be a father and his son.

I stood there, not knowing what to say. Without waiting for me to talk, the child opened his book and began to speak about his religion. He was a Jehovah's Witness.

I hadn't had a visit from a Jehovah's Witness for years, and my first thought was to politely thank them for coming, tell them I was very busy, and close the door. But for some reason, I couldn't. I just stood there, listening to the little boy talk about how God loves me. And as I listened, I noticed something. The father was gently and firmly supporting his son as he spoke. The man's eyes were filled with admiration for his son. The boy was a bit nervous; at intervals he paused and stammered slightly. And each time this happened, his father gently squeezed his shoulder giving him encouragement and support. I also noticed the father was wearing strong thick-soled black work shoes with a shine to them – shoes just like the ones my father had worn when I was this boy's age.

I opened the door wider and listened patiently to them for a long time. When the boy finally reached a stopping point, I excused myself and went to get a ten-dollar bill from my wallet. I returned to the door, passed it to the child, and thanked him for his time. I looked up at his father and thanked him as well. They seemed pleased, and they turned to go on their way.

I closed the door and watched as they passed my living room window. Then I returned to my desk and sat back down to continue writing about my "daddy" issues. Seconds later, I was dumbstruck by thoughts of what had just happened at my front door.

I'd been so eager to get back to work and finish the darn paper that I hadn't appreciated the true impact of what had just transpired. But now it came rolling over me like a freight train: the love in the father's eyes as his son spoke, his expression of admiration, his hand on his son's shoulder in a gesture of affection and support.

I was now filled with enormous pain because I'd never received such support and admiration from my own father. I had missed out on the love that such a father could give to a son. I sat with these feelings for some time and then, with a flash of insight, I understood that although I had felt abandoned by my father, ultimately it was I who had abandoned myself. I was suddenly overwhelmed with intense love both for myself and for my father. All of my issues with my father were now transformed into a deep sense of compassion for him, and I knew that he had loved me in the best way that he knew how.

I felt a strong gratitude toward the young boy and his father who had come to my door. I thought of how I'd wanted to dismiss them quickly, and how grateful I was that I hadn't. And in that moment I forgave my father for any failings, and I released all my misperceptions that he should have been anything other than what he was.

I had received a greater gift than the simple experience of having a father and son knock on my door: God had answered my prayer. I took a deep sigh of relief, confident that I had now experienced the profound love a father could have for his son. And I was grateful that this had opened my heart to feelings of compassion for my father, who had done the best he could.

CHAPTER 19

Remembering

Memory was a curse, yes, he thought, but it was also the greatest gift.
Because if you lose memory you lose everything.
    ~ Anne Rice

Years ago in the 1980s I saw a movie called *The Mission*. The film is about the experiences of Father Gabriel, a Spanish Jesuit priest (played by Jeremy Irons), who has come to South America in the 1750s to build a mission for the indigenous people living in the jungle. The other main character is Rodrigo Mendoza (played by Robert DeNiro), a Spanish mercenary soldier who kidnaps the natives and sells them as slaves. After Mendoza murders his brother, Father Gabriel challenges him to atone for his sins by accompanying the priests on their trip into the jungle. The penance is that as Mendoza travels, he must drag behind him a heavy bundle containing his armor and his sword.

The film made an impression on me when I saw it, but I had mostly forgotten it by the time I was in my second year of graduate school in Santa Monica. One weekend I arrived as usual for my classes, and although I felt happy seeing fellow students, I was, as usual, fatigued by the ordeal of commuting from Sedona to Los Angeles for another weekend of intensive classes that lasted for many hours. On this occasion, as I prepared for my Saturday classes, all I could think about was how great it would be relax at the beach and chill out.

I was committed to earning my master's degree in spiritual psychology, but on this particular weekend I was really fed up. Sometimes the classes involved self-exploration, or listening to the self-explorations of classmates. On this particular day, after hours of morning classes, I'd had enough. By the time the afternoon break arrived, I was ready to walk into the classroom and proclaim to the founders/ professors, sitting in the front of the auditorium and everyone else, "The hell with all of your emotionalism. I've had it with this drama!"

But when I returned from the afternoon break, the professors announced that we would be watching a movie.

Meanwhile, in spite of my resistance on that particular day, up to this point I'd been working very hard to let go of my destructive beliefs and patterns. I'd come to realize that in my subconscious, love and pain were tightly intertwined. Similarly, I'd let go of the belief that I had to be poor to be spiritual. In addition, I believed on some level that if I loved someone, that person would die or otherwise abandon me. Given my family history – my brother's death and my mother's mental illness – this made perfect sense to me intellectually. Now, it would soon make sense on an emotional level, as well.

The movie began to play, and to my surprise it was *The Mission*, the Robert DeNiro film I'd seen decades earlier. But this time, my experience as I viewed the film was totally different. I watched DeNiro playing the soldier Mendoza, and as he dragged his armor behind him I felt as though I were being ripped wide open. Nevertheless, I knew I needed to watch what was on the screen. All my previous impatience with the class, as well as my desire to go relax on the beach, went right out of my mind.

The film's scenes unfolded before my eyes, and I keenly felt this movie's message being transmitted into my soul and heart. On-screen, Mendoza was going through his ordeal, hauling his heavy armor through the jungle, several times almost resulting in his own death. And as I watched, I recognized a pattern that was deeply entrenched inside me. Like Mendoza, I was carrying a lot of weighty baggage.

At one point in the film, the priests and Mendoza encounter a little boy among the natives in the jungle. The child, with a smile on his face and in a moment of playfulness, raises a machete and brings it down, severing the rope that ties Mendoza to the heavy burden of his armor.

In that moment, as the young boy cut Mendoza's rope, I felt my own rope – the one that tied me to my own baggage – being cut as well.

Gasping for breath as I watched the on-screen film in tandem with my own film playing out inside my mind, I realized that the little boy inside of me had released me from my own baggage.

I also realized in that moment that I no longer needed to carry my brother's death or my mother's mental illness, dragging them with me as Mendoza had dragged his heavy armor. I had suffered enough at my own hand. And it was now clear that loving someone didn't mean they would die or abandon me. I was enough, and watching the film had taught me this lesson of self-love.

The cord that for so many years had tied me to this dreadful baggage had been severed forever, and I was now free of a terrible burden.

CHAPTER 20

The Winged People
and the Sacred Medicine Wheel

Medicine Wheel: A circle of cobble stones built by Native Americans . . . having astronomical/calendrical, ceremonial, memorial, or spiritual significance
    ~ Dictionary.com

I was preparing for a speech, writing, and making a huge poster as a visual aid. It depicted the sacred Medicine Wheel.

The Medicine Wheel is a Native American monument often associated with the Plains Indian tribes in the U.S. and Canada. Made of stones arranged on the ground, in most forms a Medicine Wheel looks like a giant four-spoked wheel, with a circle of stones crossed by intersecting lines. Four lines of rocks radiate from the center, and these point to the four directions: the East, South, West, and North.

On the poster, I was creating the quadrant that symbolizes the East.

I was more than a little nervous about my upcoming presentation. It was important to me to do a good job of sharing information about the Medicine Wheel. But would I be able to get the information across? Could I make my points effectively in a way that would help others?

The previous evening my teacher Grandfather Morning Owl and I had enjoyed one of his delicious home-cooked meals as we'd discussed healing modalities, his life's experiences, and my "public speaking anxiety" about the speech. Grandfather brought up Black Elk – a Lakota Nation elder who wrote *The Sacred Ways of a Lakota* in which he shares information about sacred Lakota rituals and ceremonies, such as the Stone People's lodge (popularly called a "sweat lodge") and the chanupa or "peace pipe" ceremony. Grandfather said, "You need to reread Black Elk's book."

Back at home later that night, I searched my bookcase and pulled out the book. Before I opened it, I asked Spirit to reveal the wisdom I needed. Then I sat down and let the book open on its own.

The chapter was called "The Eagle." I was grateful because I've always felt close to birds – whom I call the "Winged People." As a child I did a lot of ceremonies with birds. Sometimes, to help them pass into the spirit world, I'd carefully bury the dead birds I found. Birds of many colors and diverse powers have revealed their wisdom to me over the years.

This evening was no different.

I finished the chapter and, feeling exhausted, went to bed full of gratitude toward the Winged People. Before falling asleep as I drifted off I prayed, "Winged People, reveal the wisdom I need in such a way that I will understand it and use it for the greatest good."

Next morning I woke up early, which was good because I still had to complete the sacred Medicine Wheel visual aid for my presentation the next day.

It was still dark. The sun wasn't up, and my clock read 4 a.m. As I rose from my bed, I realized the Winged People hadn't revealed anything to me in my dreams. But for some reason I was fine with that. In fact, I felt grateful.

I sat down to work on the presentation poster, and I heard a voice in my head saying, "Get this project done." I was still drawing the East quadrant, the one that signifies the golden warm yellow morning sun, new beginnings, and the spirit animal of the eagle. As I worked, I asked Spirit, "Will this sacred Medicine Wheel be part of my healing and facilitating work with others? Will my speech go well? Am I on the right path?" Almost immediately I heard that small voice inside of me: "Look outside the window." And sure enough, the warm yellow morning sun was there quite literally, streaming from the East through my picture window and lighting up the poster board in front of me.

What's more, highlighted in the warm rays, perched a few feet outside my window, was a red-tailed hawk. Full of gratitude, I thanked the hawk for coming, and I thanked the Winged People for their loving support and wisdom throughout my life. Then I heard my inner voice once more: "Go to the kitchen window."

Peering out the window of my kitchen, I did not see a hawk . . . I saw three of them, perched majestically in the nearby willow! They were assembled in a triangle, one several feet above the others, and all three were staring right at me. Seeing them was so overwhelming that the experience took my breath away. In fact, I couldn't move for several minutes as I took in their presence.

After some time the hawks flew away, and I went back to work on the poster. But again I heard that little voice. This time it said, "Is this really the right path for me?" As soon as that thought occurred I noticed that one of the hawks had returned. The message I got was loud and clear, as if this hawk were literally speaking to me and saying "Get back to writing!" I felt almost like a child being admonished in a loving parental way.

I finished preparing for my presentation, and I caught a plane that night for Los Angeles. The next day I gave my Medicine Wheel talk in a state of utter calmness, without a bit of nervousness, confident that the spirit world and the Winged People were always present and helping me. From the beginning of the presentation, I could feel the presence of those who had gone before me and those who are yet to come. I concluded by saying, "Today the Medicine Wheel is a symbol of peaceful interactions and harmonious connections among all beings on Mother Earth."

The applause was deafening. Many people came up to me afterward and told me what a great job I'd done. Others said how impressed they were with the wisdom I'd imparted to them, and how helpful it was. I left feeling great about myself, my speech, and the invaluable opportunity to help others by sharing information about the sacred Medicine Wheel.

Thank you, Winged People!

CHAPTER 21

Red Tailed Hawk

A red-tailed hawk rose high on an air current, calling out shrill, sequential
rasps of raptor joy.
   ~ Barbara Kingsolver

I've had many Winged People encounters, and one took place last Tuesday at the home of a landscaping client.

I had entered her curved driveway from a different direction than the one I usually took. Previously I'd always entered from the North. But last Tuesday, for some reason, a voice told me to enter it another way – from the East.

I put the truck in park, got out, and went to get my landscaping tools from the back. As I did, I noticed a large opening in my client's huge red-tipped photinia bush.

And there it was.

It was a young red-tailed hawk.

Birds are messengers, and I knew immediately that there was a message in this experience. But it would be several days before I'd understand its meaning.

I stepped closer to the hawk, and I saw that it wasn't moving. It had just died, and as in life, its talons still tightly clenched the plant's branches.

The way of the world being what it is, I knew that if I left it there, soon Mother Earth's other creatures would treat it with disrespect.

So I decided to remove the hawk's earthly body from the plant. I carefully unclenched the young hawk's talons from the branches. I lifted it from its perch, and its muscles and tendons were warm and soft to my touch. As I gently laid the body in the bed of my truck, I felt a deep sense of reverence and awe.

The next day I called a Lakota friend, Joseph Grey Wolf, to ask what I should do with the hawk. I wanted to treat this bird with deepest respect and to help its spirit depart from this world. Joseph met me at dusk at my landscaping yard. We prayed for the young hawk's spirit and sang a Lakota song.

Joseph asked me to call the hawk by its name in my native Cherokee tongue. I did and repeated several times, "Ah-ni-tsi-sk-wa, Ah-ni-tsi-sk-wa, Ah-ni-tsi-sk-wa. Aho, Aho, Aho."

Joseph told me that the wisdom of the hawk was coming into my life. I didn't know what this meant, but I accepted his words without question. He told me to bury the hawk the following day.

The next morning as I was at my computer, I became frustrated because my printer wouldn't work. I backed off from the machines and from the frustrations, and I simply sat there with my emotions.

After a few minutes, the thoughts came into my mind of a man who wanted to know about my experiences and how to make similar things happen for him.

With these thoughts, a sense of sadness overcame me. I realized that I was like this young hawk that had just died. I envisioned myself telling this man that I have died many times, that I will die again and again, and that only by dying can one grasp the essence of existence.

That is one of the great mysteries of life: to live, to die, and again to rise from the ashes with a newly awakened wisdom and expanded knowledge. The pains and joys of life are beyond words, but we must endure what life gives us in order to open our hearts.

I thought of the story of the guru and his student. The student wanted to know what it was like to love God with all of his being, and the guru agreed to teach him. They walked to the river, and the guru plunged his devotee's head under water. He held the student's head under water for so long that when he finally allowed the young man to come up for air, the student was gasping and sputtering. As the student looked at the guru in anger and disbelief, the guru said, "When you wish to know God as much as you wish for your next breath, then you will know God."

I knew that the time had come to bury the hawk, so I left my computer and printer to prepare the bird for burial. The experience reminded me of the many times in my childhood when I'd buried the bodies of dead birds.

I opened the new red flannel cloth that Joseph had instructed me to use, and I placed the hawk in the center of it. I folded it into quarters over the young bird, and I tied it with four blue ribbons signifying the four directions. I drove to a holy canyon in Sedona, and as I placed the sacred bundle high up in a large juniper tree with feelings of honor, love, and gratitude, I said a prayer to Spirit while giving thanks to the majestic hawk for its wisdom.

The next day something magical happened. I was driving up Oak Creek Canyon to fill my bottles with fresh water from the aquifer. As I drove, a small colorful hummingbird hovered right in front of my windshield. It lingered for a second or two, and then in a flash it flew off to my left across the windshield. And if that wasn't enough of a thrill, as I was driving back home, an eagle flew just a few feet in front of me with its wings fully outstretched.

When I got home, eager to see what medicine and messages these birds were sharing with me, I raced to my bookshelf and pulled out *Animal Speak* by Ted Andrews. I found that the hummingbird signifies "tireless joy and the nectar of life." I read on. The hummingbird tells us to take joy in what we do and to "sing it out," according to Andrews. The hummingbird also generates a kind of "internal massage" to bring us health and balance. Andrews added that hummingbirds are "fiercely independent."

I allowed these words to soak in. And then I thumbed through the chapters to the section on eagles. I found that eagles represent "illumination of spirit, healing, and creation." Specifically, according to Andrews, they teach us to be on the earth but not of it.

Because I'd been on a journey to get water that morning, I delved further into the book to see if Andrews said anything about water and eagles. Lo and behold he did. Andrews wrote that because water is a creative source of life, living near natural water sources is vital to the health of those (such as myself) with a bald eagle as a totem. He also wrote about the need to show control in working with the emotions and with psychic powers, and in all aspects of spirituality.

I closed the book and sat meditating on the hawk, the hummingbird, and the eagle, and how each has a special meaning for us if we are willing to uncover it.

CHAPTER 22

Messages and Messengers

*I decided that it was not wisdom that enabled poets to write their poetry,
but a kind of instinct or inspiration, such as you find in seers and prophets
who deliver all their sublime messages without knowing in the least what
they mean.*

~ Socrates

Birds, bees, snakes, and rabbits repeatedly come into my life, bringing me hope, encouragement, and wisdom. These creatures are messengers asking me to be open and aware of developments in my life.

For example, a month ago I was enjoying tea on my back porch. It was a cool morning, and a refreshing breeze was blowing. As I sat there and wondered how best to get started with my counseling work, I looked up and saw a beautiful red-tailed hawk perched ten feet away in a shaggy bark juniper tree. This was an unusual perch for a hawk because there was so little room for it. Moreover, I hadn't heard it land.

The hawk stared directly at me as if it had been waiting for me to look up. I said a few soft words to the bird, and as I spoke it lifted its right foot. It held its foot outstretched toward me, opened and closed the talons slowly, and then rested it back down on the branch.

We sat there for several minutes communicating silently with each other. And then it leaned its head and chest forward, extended its wings fully, tucked its talons beneath its body, and took flight. In its wake I felt a surge of wind blow across my face. I said goodbye to the beautiful messenger and gave thanks to it for greeting me and acknowledging my request that morning.

Another visitor gave me inspiration was when I was going through one of the toughest challenges of my life. I was struggling with trying to balance work and school as I pursued a master's degree at a program in California. I was considering leaving the university because the weekend travel, the financial burdens, and the studying seemed too much to bear while I was working full time.

One day as I sat on my back porch deliberating the pros and cons of dropping out of school, a severe rainstorm raged outside. The rain poured down all around my covered patio, and suddenly there was a small grey bird with yellow and red marks under and around its neck and head. It landed in a tree that was waving in the strong wind, branches blowing and swaying back and forth. I was amazed at how the bird had flown so calmly amid the storm. Yet there it was, holding onto the branch as though it were no big deal. It even began to sing for a moment or two, and then with another gust of wind, as quickly as it came, it flew away.

At that moment I sensed that I, too, could weather the stresses of school and work.

Another sign appeared last summer when I was cutting back a butterfly bush at a rental property. The bush was full of bees. The bees were all around my head and arms as I reached in to do the trimming. I sent the bees my positive thoughts, for I was happy to hear them busy at work – just like I was. I felt comforted and my thoughts went back to a book entitled *The Fifth Sacred Thing* that I'd read just a few months earlier, from which I had learned about the Bee People and their medicine.

Previously when I'd encountered bees I'd swatted them and said things like "Leave or I'll squash you." But this time their presence was comforting. The book had made the point that bees are powerful creatures. Now I thought about how their honey could clean and heal wounds, and how they, too, have a consciousness and a potent medicine. At that moment I gave thanks to them and realized how important they are.

Instead of resenting the hard work I was doing, I felt at peace knowing the Bee People were there, working alongside of me. I actually liked the idea that, as I stuck my arms into the bushes, they were buzzing all around me as if they were talking to me.

I went a step further and asked the Bee People to help me take more pleasure in my work. I also asked them to give me a sign that they'd heard me. But as I kept trimming those bushes, nothing happened. I decided their presence would have to be enough in that moment.

When I got home that evening I went through my usual routine, threw my work clothes into the laundry room, drank some fluids to rehydrate myself, and took a warm Epsom-salt bath to ease my sore muscles. Then I got dressed and headed out to a restaurant for dinner.

At the restaurant Jessica, the owner, came over to talk with me. We each were talking about what kind of day we'd had when she stopped me in mid-sentence and said, "Oh, how precious." With those words she reached out and lifted a little brown-and-yellow bumble bee that had been resting on my left shoulder. I grinned and mentally gave thanks to the Bee People for their spiritual support.

Perhaps the most important messengers are the guardian angels who watch over us. A few years ago I was at one of my favorite hiking places: Fay Canyon below Bear Mountain in Coconino County. I love the drive on the way there along Dry Creek Road, through one of the most scenic areas in Sedona. I also love the short and easy hike, and the natural arch and prehistoric Indian ruins along the way. This area has a special meaning for me because it was where I took one of my first hikes in Sedona when I abandoned the corporate world.

About half a mile into the hike there's a rock formation that reaches up fifty feet to the sky with a huge and heavy overhang. To me that rock formation looks like an anvil, and every time I would walk under it the question that would pop into my head was: "When will the anvil overhang fall off?"

On this particular summer afternoon I was hiking in my usual way: going moderately fast through the shaggy bark junipers and scrub oaks, and then slowing down to take in the scenic views as the sunlight shifts and moves. This day was different, however. Instead of racing past the junipers and oaks, I sat down.

I perched on a good-sized red boulder, looked at the cliffs above, and listened to the birds singing. After about three minutes I suddenly heard what sounded like a freight train roaring through the canyon. This strange noise was unnerving, and I decided to abandon my hike and head back to the car.

Two days later I returned to the canyon. There I was shocked to see that the overhang of the anvil had fallen. Massive boulders, as big as six feet in diameter, had crashed onto the trail from up above. If I'd been hiking as intended, I'd have been squashed beneath them like a bug. But my guardian angel had told me to sit down, so I hadn't been right underneath when they fell. Spirit had saved my life.

I stood there for some time, soaking in the thought of how lucky I'd been. I placed my hands on my heart. Then I looked up to the heavens and gave thanks.

CHAPTER 23

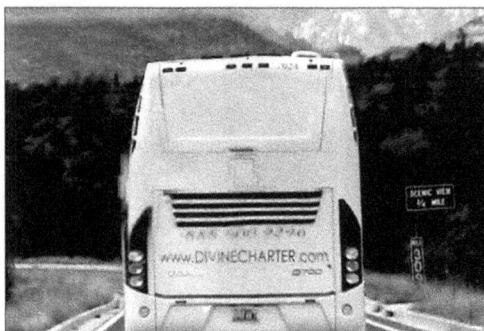

SIGNS OF HOPE

Learn from yesterday, live for today, hope for tomorrow.
~ Albert Einstein

When I'm caught up in my human limitations and judgments swirl in my head, signs of hope appear to comfort me. These signs may come as a song, as words or phrases that leap from the pages of a book, or as scenes from a movie. I refer to these moments as "singing with the angels." At these times I know I need to listen with an open heart – the expression "All you have to do is get out of the way" comes to mind.

One moment of hope came to me on a blazing hot summer day. It was 103 degrees and I was outside doing landscaping. As I worked alone in the heat and the dirt, I thought of how I'd lost my tobacco shop, the business that had allowed me to spend summer days in air-conditioned comfort meeting and talking to fascinating people from around the world. I longed to return to those days, and due to the heat and a little dehydration, I felt dejected and critical of myself for not keeping that business alive. To make things worse, I was low on cash. I had no idea how I'd pay that month's bills.

I rallied enough to tell Spirit I'd do whatever was necessary to earn the needed money. I tried to replace my feelings of fear with the trust that I'd be provided for, as I'd been so many times in the past.

As I grumbled and dug in the dirt, my cell phone rang. The caller wanted me to bid on a landscaping job. He and his wife needed a design for an area of raw space. They intended to install 3,000 square feet of pavers and 100 feet of cinderblock walls, plus underground electric and irrigation systems.

A short time later I stood in his backyard surveying the space. This would be a huge project, bigger than anything I'd done in the past, and I questioned whether I could handle it. I wanted to say no, but something inside wouldn't let me walk away. I knew in my heart that I could do a far better job than anyone else they'd find. As I looked at the site, I visualized what was needed. More importantly, I trusted that Spirit would pick up the slack.

So with great feelings of hope I went home and created a design. It still seemed almost too much to handle. But I was determined. In addition, I confess that I was afraid of being broke. So I proceeded. A few days later when I presented the proposal to my clients, my mind was full of nagging thoughts such as, "Will they like it?" and "Is it too expensive for them?"

We sat at their kitchen table, and I explained in detail my vision of what I wanted to create for them. They looked at me with joyful smiles saying, "Great! We love it! How much is the deposit?"

Mentally I gave a deep sigh of relief as they wrote me a check for $7,000 for the first installment.

Driving home that afternoon, I felt great. And I thanked Spirit for coming through for me, for giving me this great opportunity to serve my new clients. I entered the circular roundabout on the way home, and my truck was suddenly sandwiched between two enormous commercial buses. One pulled into the roundabout before me and the other followed right behind me. I looked at the words printed on the buses, and I saw, written there in bold black letters: DIVINE CHARTER. In that moment I felt permeated with joy and gratitude. With a $7,000 check in my pants pocket, I realized I was being escorted home by a "DIVINE CHARTER"!

Two months later a second sign of hope reinforced my trust that I will be provided for. For weeks I'd been hearing a song in my head that's been with me since I was sixteen. It's from a symphony by Aaron Copeland called *Appalachian Spring*. This piece of music stirred my soul and helped me through many teenage challenges. As a teen I'd often played the tape in my car, and I wore it out by listening to it so much. Now, hearing the music inside my head, I remembered how my older brother had recited the words to me, saying it was an old Shaker hymn.

I later found the words in a book by Wayne Muller called *Legacy of the Heart*:

> *'Tis a gift to be simple, 'tis a gift to be free,*
> *'Tis a gift to come down to where we ought to be,*
> *And when we find ourselves in a place just right,*
> *We will be in the valley of love and delight.*

Now it was Monday morning and as I bent to prune an evergreen bush hugging the ground, I felt a profound sense of accomplishment. I was in a peaceful place mentally, and I knew I'd made a huge leap from the frustration of doing landscaping work to feelings of joy and peace. With these thoughts in my mind, a faint humming caught my attention. Could it be? I strained to listen, and I heard the familiar tune. I stood to see where the music was coming from, and there sat a young sandy-brown-haired ten-year-old boy in his front yard humming the Shaker hymn.

I stood there with a huge smile on my face listening to the boy. I was transported back to my youth and to the peace the song gave me. I placed my hand on my heart and thanked Spirit for this moment.

A third experience of hope and encouragement came to me through the guitarist Michael Hedges. He was on the cutting edge for his time, with his technique of strumming and thumping the strings of his guitar to produce a unique sound.

As a teenager back in the seventies I went to one of his concerts. That night I was late for the show, and as I ran through the back parking lot I bumped into a guy with long, frizzy, sandy-brown hair. When the concert started and Michael came out onto the stage and I realized that the guy I'd bumped into was the star, Michael Hedges!

Unfortunately he died at a very early age. I was bothered by his death because it meant I'd never hear any new music from him.

So I listened over and over to all of his songs, and through the years his music took on a deep meaning for me as, for example, his tonal quality and style comforted me through the heartaches and the lonely aftermath of a relationship.

Recently at Unity Spiritual Center a guitarist played for us, and I knew I was hearing a new piece of music influenced by Michael's work. I was so moved that tears welled up in my eyes, and I later shared with the musician how much he sounded like Michael. I was rewarded when the guitarist smiled back at me and said, "Michael Hedges has been a profound influence in my life and my music."

Later I attended a concert in Cottonwood, Arizona, by Pierre Bensusan, a French guitarist from Paris. I had gone simply because I wanted to hear what kind of guitar music a Parisian would make, and I was blown away by the performance. Once again I heard Michael's influence coming from the guitar. This was at a time when I'd just split up with Sarah, the woman of my dreams, and I was grateful that Pierre and Michael were there to comfort me in my moments of sadness. When Pierre took a break, I spoke with him and learned that Michael had been a good friend of his. He dedicated a song to Michael in his next set.

Michael came to me once more when I was recently in Santa Monica after traveling to Big Sur to search for a new home and a place to establish my retreat center. I was frustrated about not finding the right spot, and I was lonely. I strolled up and down a busy street near the Santa Monica pier asking Spirit to show me where my next home would be. Many people were on the street, but I was alone and a sense of loneliness overwhelmed me. As I continued walking that Friday evening, the sun faded into darkness and I felt I was just killing time rather than doing anything productive. I felt disconnected from the path I was trying to take, the path of offering retreats and serving humanity.

As I rounded the corner to the Third Street Promenade and moved past the store windows, I heard someone strumming a guitar. Instantly I felt better, and I smiled because Michael's music was filling the air. I sat down on a bench a few feet from the guitarist, and I leaned back, feeling a warmth in my chest and my heart beating. I listened for quite a while with a pleasant sense of connectedness to Michael, and I knew the music was being sent to me by him and by his namesake, the Archangel Michael.

Spirit had given me another sign that everything would be okay. I was no longer alone. I was connected. I would find my new home. I would find exactly the right place to establish a retreat center. I would productively serve my fellow humans. I let go of all fear and doubt about needing to know where I was supposed to live and work. Just hearing Michael's music in that moment was enough.

With a renewed sense of hope and joy I approached the guitarist. I dropped a twenty-dollar bill in his container to pay for one of the CDs he was selling. At that moment, another man approached the musician and said, "You sound so much like Michael Hedges." I was delighted to know I wasn't the only one who'd thought this. Then the man asked, "Do you know who he is?"

The guitarist replied, "No, I don't." But that didn't matter to me. Clutching my new CD, I headed back to my hotel room, happy as a lark.

CHAPTER 24

ARCHANGEL GABRIEL

*You don't need a formal prayer or invocation to call angels to your side.
Simply think, "Angels, please surround me," and there they are..*
~ *Doreen Virtue*

On January 11, 2011 (1/11/11!), I had a profoundly mystical
experience.
Early that morning I was meditating as I typically do each day. As
my meditation CD played calming and peaceful sounds, I requested
divine guidance in writing the book that the archangels were nudging
me to create. I wanted not only to share my story, but to assist others
in releasing negative behavior patterns so they could rediscover their
authentic selves and live the lives their souls had intended when they
had entered this lifetime.

Writing this book was a challenge for me. Part of me believed that
no one would read it. I also feared exposing myself in its pages, and I
felt very vulnerable. These feelings led to procrastination; maybe if I
procrastinated long enough, I'd just forget all about writing the book
and never have to face my fears? Meanwhile, I felt as if a part of me
were dying, and I connected that feeling to writing the book. But on
the other hand, perhaps it was all good. Maybe if I could be ready,
even excited, to let go, I would make room for new and better aspects
of the self.

As I went deeper into the meditation on this day something

extreme began to happen. I felt a pair of huge white wings growing and expanding behind me, unfolding and filling two thirds of my meditation room, and I felt my heart expanding into the rest of the room. My heart was guiding me forward into the unknown, and I felt safe and loved.

I sat in this experience for several minutes. As I felt an energy filling me and filling the room, I heard a voice from inside of me saying, "Archangel Gabrielle." The name was the female form, and the presence was that of a female aspect of the Archangel Gabriel. I wasn't sure what to say or do. But I knew I was surrounded by strength, guidance, and love.

I was stunned that such a powerful angel would visit me. And I didn't know what to do with the experience. So after I came back into my body from the meditative state, I thanked her for appearing in response to my prayers. I was thrilled about the experience, and I felt that the visitation was enough. That afternoon I shared what had happened with my girlfriend Sarah, and in her excitement she said, "Do some research to find out more about what Archangel Gabrielle is trying to tell you."

I remembered from my Catholic upbringing that all angels named in the Bible are male. I also recalled that Archangel Gabriel was the male messenger who announced to Mary that she'd conceived and was carrying the Son of God in her womb. But I didn't know much more than that.

Later that night I awoke at 2 a.m. with Archangel Gabriel on my mind. I got up, went to my computer, entered "Archangel Gabriel" as a search term, and began to scan Websites. As I did this I asked, "Spirit, please reveal to me that which is for the highest good."

One Website was titled "Archangel Gabriel: Messenger from God." The URL was http://suite101.com/a/archangel-gabriel-a106219, and I clicked on it. There I learned that Archangel Gabriel is sometimes depicted as a female; indeed, throughout the site Gabriel was referred to as "she."

At the Website was a beautiful artist's rendering of Archangel Gabriel. And right below the picture was my name! The words read "Archangel Gabriel Sends Messages of Love – Kevin Rosseel." I asked myself, what are the chances that my name, Kevin, would appear anywhere on the page, let alone under the picture of Archangel Gabriel? I scrolled through the next two pages, reading the material, and I was even more astonished because ninety percent of what I saw was right on target with what I was dealing with in my life. All of the points listed as Archangel Gabriel's specialties were directly related to things that were happening to me.

The Website covered the principles of the Spiritual Law of Intervention on one's behalf. One principle is that angels won't intervene in our lives uninvited, so we must be sure to ask for angelic assistance when we need it. Another principle is that angels can intervene if we are about to die prematurely, before our time is up according to the sacred contract with the Divine. In such instances, archangels will protect us uninvited because in such situations we might be incapable of asking for help.

I next found the following quote from Shanta Gabriel: "Archangel Gabriel is a messenger from God and a link to the communication of truth, harmony, and balance within all beings." This quotation was profoundly meaningful to me, because much of my life has been about finding a balance between the material and spiritual worlds. By now my heart was pounding. Everything I was reading was directly related to my life, my challenges, and the visitation I'd experienced the previous day.

I scrolled down further, and I found a passage about creative writing, which directly related to the creation of my book. The words on the screen before me read: "Gabriel, as a messenger angel, assists writers and journalists so that their work brings healings and blessings to the world." This was one of my hopes for my book.

As I read through that Website, I felt a deep sense of gratitude not just for the visitation from Archangel Gabriel, but for being sent the guidance I'd requested during my meditation. One part of the site referred to nurturing the inner child, another important theme in my life. And this wisdom became particularly relevant to me a few days later when I had an intense and disturbing dream.

I dreamed about a painting by the great Spanish artist Francisco Goya. I'd found the image horrific when I'd first seen it, and now it had entered my dream world. It was the painting titled *Saturn Devouring His Son*. In Roman mythology, the god Saturn (called Cronos by the Greeks) was the ruler of the universe. Afraid of being overthrown by his son, Saturn ate the child immediately after birth, and Goya's painted image showed this act.

The dream was appropriate. At that time my critical and self-judging inner tyrant was reigning supreme over my daily life. It was devouring my inner child, just as Saturn devoured his own son in the painting. At times I could be my own worst enemy, but as I was pursuing my master's degree in spiritual psychology, I'd increasingly been in touch with my inner child. So as troubling as it was, I took the dream to be a clear sign that I should be gentler with myself and less critical.

A few days later, I had an experience that reinforced my belief that Archangel Gabriel was present with me on a daily basis. I was attending a lecture at Unity Spiritual Center, and during a break I stood in line for the restroom. While waiting I had a conversation with an elderly woman, and I shared my experience with Archangel Gabriel. When I finished she spoke, with her eyes glowing and looking directly into mine: "My name is Gabriella." Goose bumps covered my body as I heard those words. Over the next day or so, I met two other people named Gabriel and Gabrielle. For days, I couldn't stop smiling and laughing with joy. Synchronicity always reminds us that our angels and spirits are always with us.

CHAPTER 25

GROWING PAINS

Find a place inside where there's joy, and the joy will burn out the pain.
~ Joseph Campbell

You might think that the experiences with Archangel Gabriel would have sent me into a writing frenzy. And it did seem that, for a while, my life moved forward with a renewed sense of direction. But then, a few weeks later, I experienced an extraordinary soreness in my shoulder blades. I couldn't raise my arms without severe pain. It felt as if someone were stabbing me with red-hot pokers, and it never let up, not even at night, so I had trouble sleeping.

I finally sought help from a chiropractor who specialized in sports medicine and who'd worked with professional athletes such as those on the Arizona Cardinals football team. After a thorough examination of my spinal column and shoulders, he looked at me with a puzzled expression and said, "In all of my twenty years of doing chiropractic work, I've never seen anything like this. I can't help you. I'm sorry." I was crushed. I didn't know what else to do. My nights were spent in sleepless pain. And there was no respite; instead of gradually getting better, the pain got worse.

A few more days passed with searing pain by day and little sleep at night, and I wondered how I'd survive this situation. I was in agony and I was exhausted. Then my girlfriend Sarah told me about a healer from the Philippines named Brother Georgio. He was in town, she was going to see him, and she insisted that I go with her to learn if he could help with my shoulder pain.

I looked at her and said, "No way. I'm not going to another healer or psychic."

"Then I'll go and check him out," she replied. "If I decide he's the real deal, I'll pay for your treatment as a gift."

I agreed to go if she determined that he was genuine.

She scheduled an appointment through Mary, his assistant, and went to see him later that day. When she returned, she was beaming from ear to ear. "You have to go see him!" she exclaimed.

Seeing her enthusiasm, I scheduled an appointment for the next day.

I went, and I sat in Mary's house (she hosted him) on her couch waiting for Brother Georgio to emerge from the back bedroom. After five minutes he appeared and asked me to follow him into the room. There, as I sat on the massage table, he appealed to God and the angels to assist in the healing that was about to happen. Then he asked about my problem. I described the agony in my shoulder blades and the sleep deprivation I'd experienced as a result of the pain. I was only about two-thirds into my description when he looked at me and said, "Would you like me to tell you what God is telling me?"

"Yes, please!"

"God has taken your wings because you don't know how to live in this world and see the beauty that is all around you."

As the words came out of his mouth I felt my body shrinking, and I began sobbing like a child. Thoughts flooded my mind: "How have I forsaken thee?" "What have I done wrong?" And "Only say the words and I will be healed." Like a son pleading to his father, I begged God for relief.

After a few moments I composed myself. I stretched out face down on the massage table. He said he would do a cupping therapy on my back.

I'd read about cupping. It's an ancient Chinese healing technique that uses lit objects, such as cotton balls, placed under a glass or a cup. When I'd read about it, I'd thought that I'd love to experience this treatment, so it was interesting that Brother Georgio suggested this healing modality.

The session ended and I thanked him for the cupping and for God's message. The therapy seemed to help a bit, but I was still in pain. I drove home feeling dazed, confused, and sad that the healing hadn't cured me.

After that, life went on, and I did what I could for the pain in my shoulders. Mass quantities of ibuprofen helped a little, and so did some stretching exercises. Meanwhile I continued to meditate daily, asking how I could make amends and heal this malady.

A few weeks later I began having lucid dreams about going to France. A little boy, a younger version of myself, appeared in my dreams, along with several old train stations. In one dream I called out to the boy, "Where are you?" He replied, "Come and find me!"

These dreams continued over several consecutive nights, and after I shared one of them with Sarah at breakfast, she looked at me and said, "You have to go to France. You're being called there."

That was a loaded sentence for me. I'd always wanted to visit France. I'd studied French in grade school and college in hopes of going there someday. And it wasn't a feeling of wanting to go there; it was more like wanting to *go back* there, even though I'd never been to France, at least not in this lifetime.

But in response to Sarah's comment, I rattled off all of the reasons why I *couldn't* go to France. I was in constant pain. I didn't sleep well. I didn't have the money for a trip to France. I didn't have the time. Two years earlier in the economic downturn, my business had failed and I'd lost my tobacco shop of eleven years and my home. I couldn't go to France now; I was busy trying to get back on my feet. I was struggling financially, like everyone else I knew. It was August 2011, the economy was not getting any better, and there were no positive signs on the horizon that things would improve soon.

But Sarah just looked at me and said with conviction in her voice, "You have to go to France. You're being guided. You must go!"

And as she spoke, I felt a deep sense that if I didn't go, I'd regret it for the rest of my life.

So I decided that somehow I'd make it happen.

To raise money for the trip, I started selling on eBay. I sold everything from my custom cowboy boot collection, to my leather jackets, to some of the collectibles I'd accumulated over eleven years of owing my tobacco shop. Because my birthday was coming up, Sarah offered to contribute some money for my trip as a birthday gift.

To my great surprise, once I decided to make the trip happen it didn't take long to raise the money. In addition to the eBay sales and Sarah's gift, I had enough frequent flyer miles to fly to Europe at no cost. I booked my flight.

As soon as I made the decision to go to France, numerous signs appeared as confirmations that I was doing the right thing. I repeatedly encountered the French language. Before this, I'd never come across anyone in Sedona who spoke French. But now, it seemed that I heard French every day. For example, one afternoon in a health food store I overheard a husband, wife, and two children talking in French. And a chill of excitement passed through my body as I heard them.

You might think that with the distraction of raising money and planning a trip to France, my pain went away. But it didn't. It continued, unabated. The universe was directing my life, and I was a willing participant, but I was still dealing with daily physical pain and nightly sleeping problems. It wasn't until much later during my time in Lourdes, France, when I was doing volunteer work, that the problems were finally resolved.

CHAPTER 26

FREEDOM

If you can't fly, then run. If you can't run, then walk. If you can't walk,
then crawl. But whatever you do, you have to keep moving forward.
  ~ Dr. Martin Luther King, Jr.

I diligently prepared for my trip to Europe. I sold things to get money for my journey. I paid bills and packed my bags. Finally, it was the day before my flight, and I checked to see that my credit cards and passport were in my waist bag. That night before going to sleep, my girlfriend asked if I'd made copies of my credit cards and passport so I'd have these in case they got lost or stolen. I hadn't even thought of doing this, so I got out of bed, went into our home office, and copied my credit cards and passport.

It felt as if my alarm went off the minute my head hit the pillow, for almost immediately it was four a.m. and time to go to the airport. A shuttle van took me the 100 miles from Sedona to Phoenix Sky Harbor. I'd thought I would sleep on the shuttle, but I was too excited.

At the airport I checked my luggage, went through TSA security without a problem, and found a nice empty chair within view of my boarding gate. I was tired yet exhilarated. I'd be seeing Europe for the first time. I'd catch a US Airways flight to Atlanta, then I'd travel via Lufthansa Airlines to Frankfurt, Germany. There I'd visit my father's homeland of Landstuhl, then on to Monaco and the French Riviera, then Lourdes, and finally a stop in the central French countryside before my final destination of Paris. Wow! It was actually happening!

I boarded the flight to Atlanta, and as I settled into my seat, I could feel the exhaustion catch up with me. The past two weeks had been hectic as I'd prepared for the trip. I'd sold my things on eBay and shipped the items. I'd purchased my Eurail train passes. I'd converted some dollars into Euros at my local bank. But more importantly, I'd completed the last segment of my two years of studies in spiritual psychology. During those final ten intense days, one of the last instructions we'd received was not to undertake any major or life-changing acts or decisions for the next month. I hadn't wanted to admit to myself that I was going against that advice with this trip; I was too excited about visiting Germany and France.

Meanwhile, everything was going smoothly – too smoothly. As the Airbus A320 lifted off, I reclined my aisle seat and fell asleep. I awoke as the wheels touched the runway in Atlanta where I'd catch my connecting flight to Frankfurt. As I approached the customs counter, I reached for my passport.

It wasn't there.

My heart was pounding as I frantically shuffled through various documents and paper money. It just wasn't there. I got out of line and in a near panic, I dumped the contents of my little waist pouch on an empty chair: no passport. Then it hit me. I'd left it in the copy machine at home. I don't think I've ever been more angry with myself.

Things went from bad to worse. I'd used US Airways frequent-flier miles to obtain my ticket from Atlanta to Frankfurt, and now I'd have to miss that flight. The Lufthansa attendant explained that I'd need to ask US Airways for a new ticket with the same frequent-flier miles, but this was not guaranteed. I was so upset that I couldn't even speak – which was a good thing, because I was ready to say something pretty nasty.

I called my girlfriend at home. She could FedEx my passport, but it was now Saturday night, and Monday was a holiday, and FedEx didn't offer holiday delivery. I couldn't get the passport sent until Tuesday morning for delivery on Wednesday. I was so frustrated that I was practically jumping out of my skin. It was all I could do not to snap at my girlfriend who was doing her best to help me.

Instead of waiting four days, I decided to fly back to Phoenix immediately and have her meet me there with my passport. As I waited for the flight, I was beside myself with anxiety and frustration. I was too upset at the time to know what I realized later: that when you're tired and stressed, don't just double-check. Take a few deep breaths, be in the current moment, and triple-check all important details of your life.

Meanwhile, my mind was full of conflicting thoughts. I was still excited about traveling in Europe. But if everything happens for a reason, what was going on here? Was Spirit telling me to go home and forget about the trip? Or was this a challenge to see if I was truly dedicated and determined? I decided, tentatively, that we can't quit when things don't go according to plan. I also realized that many of the best things in my life have come out of what looked at first like adversity.

I was still too anxious to sit, so I paced up and down the international terminal. Slowly my mind moved away from my predicament, and my surroundings came back into focus. I noticed some displays honoring Dr.. Martin Luther King with various photos and other memorabilia.

I paced around the displays, and I read about King's life and philosophies. The common theme was freedom and respect for cultural and personal differences. One particular display case was titled "Freedom." As I absorbed the message, a lifetime of conditioning seemed to be torn away. Like a quick-change artist in a break-away costume, I was suddenly stripped bare, and I felt my own level of freedom. Like most kids in America, I'd learned about Dr. King as a child, and his words had cycled through my mind periodically. But now, at this moment in the Atlanta airport, frustrated about having to miss my flight and having to pay extra money, I suddenly got his message at the soul level.

As I paced around looking at the display, I recalled what had happened recently with two of my classmates. One was Palestinian, and one was Israeli. Hussein, the Palestinian, is Muslim, and Levi, the Israeli, is a Hasidic Jew. One day in class we were each to make a presentation. Levi's was almost a comedy routine, poking good-natured fun at his family and his background. He ended by extending his arms to Hussein and saying that he loved him. Hussein went up on stage and they hugged, leaving behind centuries of ethnic differences. Their act of dropping cultural hatreds felt miraculous to me that day, and their reconciliation brought about a healing for everyone in the room. As Levi and Hussein hugged, in my mind I heard Dr.. Martin Luther King's voice and words: "I have a dream." I also heard the ancient quotation: "If the mountain won't come to Muhammad, then Muhammad must go to the mountain." In that moment, I truly experienced those words and they became a part of me.

Now, as I stood in the Atlanta airport reading Dr. King's speeches, I felt a transformation. Over the next several minutes, I let his message fill my consciousness. But the relief was only momentary, and soon my concerns about my situation returned with a vengeance. I was still conflicted. I still wondered if not having my passport was an ill omen, or a message that I should cancel my trip. The pros and cons churned in my mind to the point that I was nearly driven mad with anxiety. I even entertained the thought, "Was I to meet Loretta Scott King and visit their home in Atlanta?"

With trembling hands, I dialed Sarah again on my cell phone. She suggested that I find the airport chapel and go there to ask for divine guidance. I didn't even know if the airport had a chapel, much less where it was, but I agreed to follow her suggestion. As we hung up, I turned around, and there, right in front of me, right beside the Martin Luther King display, was the chapel!

I entered and I prayed. It was hard to stay with my prayers, given my emotional state, but I sat in silence and waited for divine guidance. What came through was an intense connection to Dr. King. I felt as if he were communicating with me then, and I still do from time to time today.

Then in a moment of clarity, I knew what I had to do: I had to get back to Phoenix, retrieve my passport, and continue my trip to Europe.

So I rebooked my flight to Frankfurt with a short layover in Charleston, South Carolina, and then caught the plane to Phoenix to meet Sarah at a hotel in Scottsdale.

I was greeted by my beautiful girlfriend, and we made the best of our few hours together. She went right to sleep, but I lay there wide-eyed for fear of missing my early morning flight. I literally stayed awake until it was time to leave for the airport.

I arrived at Sky Harbor the next morning and boarded the plane. As soon as I plunked my tired body into the seat, I released the sheer exhaustion and mental fatigue of the previous thirty-six hours. I fell into a deep and peaceful sleep as Martin Luther King's words echoed in my mind: "I have a dream."

CHAPTER 27

FRANKFURT

Frankfurt am Main, commonly known as Frankfurt, is the largest city in
the German state of Hesse and the fifth-largest city in Germany.
  ~ Wikipedia

I was on my way to Frankfurt and feeling excited and anxious. I settled into the aisle seat, and the flight attendant brought me a glass
of water. The way she held it made me take notice: her right hand
cupped the side of the glass, and her left hand was opened flat with the
base of the glass resting on it. I felt as if I were being offered a chalice
of sacred water.

I recalled what had happened the night before, with forgetting my
passport and missing my flight. I'd had to go back to Phoenix. I'd had
to pay for a new airline ticket, a hotel in Phoenix, and cab fare from
and to the airport. It had cost me five hundred dollars, which was
twenty-five percent of the money I had for the trip.

My mind struggled with the attachments in my life: to my girlfriend,
to my existence, to money, to the ways I present myself to myself and
others. Over my lifetime I'd constantly criticized myself for my own
behaviors, beliefs, perceptions, and judgments. But now I was allowing
thoughts and experiences to open me fully to who I was becoming, just
as a painter selects the next vibrant color to be placed on the tip of a
brush and laid onto a blank canvas. I assured myself that I'd be okay
and that I should trust in Spirit.

With these thoughts, I slipped into a sense of peace. I was confident I didn't have to do anything more than what I was doing in that moment. I felt as if I had "rebirthed" myself into a new person: one ever present in the moment, and one who had released all attachments and preconceived ideas. Well, at least for that moment.

My mind focused on my destination, and my thoughts wandered into the Black Forest of Europe. I pictured green foliage, nature, and the serenity of animals. Yet even in that moment I was struggling to be free from the constraints I'd spent my whole life adapting. In making this trip with so little money, I was pushing through my comfort zones. I heard a little voice inside me saying, "You're pushing to the outer limits – keep going."

My mind rushed back to the Martin Luther King display I'd seen in Atlanta. I heard the words and the voice of Martin Luther King: "Break free!" And I felt my own emancipation.

The flight took on its own simplicity, and I felt more at ease. I remember eating a carrot: as I bit into it I sensed its basic nature and experienced the taste of the soil that had held it as it grew. The carrot's solid crunch nourished me beyond its simple texture. And then I felt the leather strap of my satchel. It was smooth and cool as it rested on my arm.

Meanwhile I noticed a young man and his girlfriend across the aisle. Her upper thigh was showing as she lay across his lap. My thoughts went to the tender touch of my girlfriend, and I was embarrassed to be having these thoughts as I glanced at the couple a second time.

Many other thoughts and feelings ran through my mind. I thought of my little sister. I remembered how I'd helped her years ago by making suggestions about how and when to ask our mother for help. Her trust was moving.

Then my mind was eased by hearing my Vedanta teacher: "Neti, Neti. . . . Not this. . . . Not that." I lay my head on my arms on the drop-down table in front of me, and I fell asleep.

Six hours into the flight, around 2 a.m., I awoke to the words and music of the song "Amazing Grace." As the words played in my head, feelings of gratitude swept over me. I soon fell back asleep.

Before I knew it the plane was touching down after its twelve-hour flight to Germany from Charleston. My friend Donna and her son greeted me as I stepped out of the terminal. We loaded my things into her BMW and began the forty-five minute drive to their home outside Frankfurt. As she drove I realized how exhausted I was – and how the one hundred miles per hour that she and everyone else was driving on the German freeway was disconcerting. I kept taking deep breaths and reassuring myself that we'd soon be at their home.

Later as we sat outside overlooking the small German town where they lived, Donna and Hans, her husband, served me a filling snack of fruit, cheese, sausage, and bread. Hans was eager to show me the town and the local sights. So the five of us piled into their small car and headed out.

The strongest memory I have of that tour was of the outposts of the Roman Empire. Hans was excited for me to see them. He exclaimed, "They were the outer limits of the Roman Kingdom!" And as he spoke, I thought of my own outer limits, and of how I was pushing beyond them. I smiled and relaxed into the car's leather seat.

Around 10 p.m. we arrived back at their home. I thanked them for the tour, climbed the stairs, and collapsed onto the bed in their guest room that doubled as an office. The solitude and quiet was what I needed. I stretched out on the bed and felt a sense of inner joy. Spending time with them, I'd seen and heard the love they had for each other. But I had a vague feeling of inner disruption at the same time. Something was brewing deep inside me.

I lay there awake for the next two hours, trying to push past my jet lag and the sadness that stirred within me. I asked God to assist me in understanding and to give me comfort. Ultimately the message from deep within was that the only person who really needed to show up for myself was me.

Other thoughts flooded my mind. I heard my inner voice say, "Face your pride and embarrassment." But what did the voice mean by "pride" and "embarrassment"? I felt a vulnerability flooding through me, and I thought about pride. Pride was something destructive and not loving. It was my pride that had built walls around me and that kept me apart from others. I had elevated myself to some higher level where I thought I was better than others. Pride was my misguided sense of superiority. And here in Europe, my pride in being an American gave me a feeling of being above others.

Next I thought about "embarrassment." I felt a deep embarrassment about my pride. I reminded myself of how little money I had, and how irresponsible it was of me to make this trip. It was embarrassing to be without sufficient funds, and it was embarrassing to feel irresponsible.

Then the emotions flooded over me. These thoughts coupled with the physical exhaustion of the trip were too much. I had to let go of whatever was holding me back from feeling centered and peaceful. I turned to stifle my sobs in the pillow because I didn't want anyone to hear me.

Earlier that evening I'd tried three times to phone my girlfriend, but I hadn't reached her. Now this, too, upset me. I knew that if I could have spoken to her I would have felt better. But whatever was happening to me emotionally was something I had to handle by myself.

Over the next half hour I began to face my pride. I saw how it had kept me from truly loving myself and how it had denied me the opportunity to be open and vulnerable, and to experience love with others. My sense of a destructive pride and superiority faded into thoughts of the loving family I was privileged to be staying with. I was sad because for most of my life I'd missed out on having a close family. In addition, I was missing my girlfriend and my son. I also realized how my hostess Donna reminded me of my little sister (named Diane), and how my host Hans had the patience of a saint.

That night I let go of my pride. I experienced my own vulnerability, and I gave up my feelings of not being enough. I released the self-limiting thought that I was better than others, and I relaxed into what this loving family had to offer me.

As with new eyes I began to see more clearly. The truth was that I was enough. I didn't have to do or be anything more than I was. And these new understandings would always be with me, no matter where I was in the world.

I knew, then, not to be afraid of my humanness or my own vulnerability. In that moment I realized that vulnerability was one of my strengths. My mind traveled back once again to the Martin Luther

King display in the Atlanta Airport, and I heard his voice say to me, "This is your road to Freedom!"

With a deep sense of peace and exhaustion I lifted the copy of the "Our Father" that I had placed on the nightstand. It was written in English that had been translated directly from Aramaic, rather than from Aramaic to Greek to Latin to English. I read the last phrase, "For you are the ground and the fruitful vision, the birth, power, and fulfillment, as all is gathered and made whole once again!" And I immediately fell into a deep and peaceful sleep.

CHAPTER 28

MY FIRST GLIMPSE OF PARIS, AND MY TRIP TO MONACO

There comes a time when you no longer speak the words, you become them, and they become you.
  ~ Joseph White Owl

The next morning Donna and her two children accompanied me to the train station forty-five minutes away. They walked me into the station, and Donna made sure I had everything I needed for my trip to Paris and Monte Carlo. Finally we hugged and said goodbye.
I was excited. I was going to Paris! It was something I'd wanted to do all my life.

As I waited for the train I realized it would pass by Landstuhl, Germany, my paternal grandmother's birthplace. I'd previously debated whether to stop and see where my father's family came from. But I'd had so little time. From Paris I'd head immediately south to visit Monaco, Lourdes, and many places in between, before finally returning to Paris. And I was trying to do all of this in twelve days with only 400 Euros.

The train to Paris wasn't leaving right away, so I stepped into the train station lounge and ordered a snack and a cup of tea. There I noticed a tree, ten feet high, growing right in the center of the lounge. Its presence comforted me. For the next half hour I enjoyed the tree and my tea, and then I headed downstairs to the tracks where my train stood waiting. I found a seat and as the train pulled out of the Frankfurt station, I glanced once more at the schedule. Again I thought about how I'd travel right past Landstuhl, and I made up my mind to visit.

As we pulled in to Landstuhl I was bursting with excitement to see where my father's family came from. I'd heard many stories about the place from my godmother, whom I called Aunt Isabelle, when I was growing up in Saint Louis. She'd gone back there to visit several times, and she always took soaps, and other simple things we took for granted, to relatives who received them as precious gifts.

Getting off the train, I hailed a cab and told the driver I wanted to see Landstuhl in the next couple of hours. We drove through the small town nestled at the foot of a mountain that had been named after my family so many generations ago. We passed the small shops that lined the street as we made our way to the Landstuhl Castle hundreds of feet above the town. On arriving at the castle, I exited the cab and asked the driver to come back for me in an hour.

I explored the remnants of the Landstuhl Castle, and I wondered what it had been like a hundred years ago. As I walked from the castle's entry to a patio restaurant that overlooked the town, I decided to see if I had any relatives still living there. I asked the waitress for a phone book, and after I placed my order I scoured the phone book for my last name. But I was disappointed because I couldn't find my name in the book. When the waitress brought my food, I asked her if she knew a town historian or anyone who knew the town's history.

To my surprise she said, "Ja! The man at that table right behind you. His family has lived here for generations."

I approached the man, explained why I was there, and asked if he knew anyone named Westrich. He thought for a while, and then he said, "Yes, I do." He said the family that owned the town bakery had that last name. He added that in the next town there was a clothing factory, and owner also shared the name.

I thanked him, turned around and looked out over the town, and realized that it was getting late. It was Sunday and none of the shops, let alone a nearby factory, would be open. So I returned to the station to catch the train for Paris. As I said goodbye to Landstuhl, I felt inside me the presence of my grandparents doing the same thing just two generations ago.

It was nearly midnight when I arrived at the train station in Paris, tired but exhilarated. I had two hours until I'd catch the train for the tiny country of Monaco to the south on the Mediterranean. So I crossed the street to a bistro where I could sit and relax until my train left.

As I waited in the bistro my enthusiasm dissipated. I'd dreamed of a "trés chic" city – Paris! – but the reality was a place where a cold drizzle fell and a loud subway rumbled along nearby. My thoughts went to home and the warm bed where my sweet girlfriend lay. The exhaustion of the trip and the late hour enveloped me. After more than an hour, I saw a man across the street locking the gates to the station. I was in shock. "Did I miss my train?" I thought. I asked a passing policeman, and he explained that the train I wanted would leave from a different station twenty minutes away.

And there was no way I could get there in time.

I decided to try to make it anyway. I carried my luggage to a bus stop where I caught a bus filled with rowdy teenagers. When we arrived at the correct train station, I navigated my way through the teens, only to see a similar pair of locked doors and a sign indicating that they wouldn't open for another four hours. Disheartened, I stood there on the street with my luggage, trying to keep warm and dry and trying to ignore the filthy toothless bums who kept approaching me. After a few hours, I had to find a spot some distance away to relieve my bladder. It wasn't fun. And it wasn't the Paris of my dreams.

At 4:45 a.m. the doors were finally unlocked. I entered and found a place to buy some fresh chocolate croissants and a cup of tea. Soon, after that awful night, I was on my way to Monaco, sitting comfortably in a first-class seat. God, I was happy!

As I went through the many stops and train transfers along the way, I realized that it was all a metaphor for life: we're exhausted, cold, tired, and confused one minute, and then comfortable and well-rested the next. In that moment I vowed to stop the frenzied pace I'd kept up during the past few years, to slow down and be present in the moment, and to "stop and smell the roses" as best I could.

Finally I reached the resort town of Monte Carlo in Monaco. I had a reservation and, asking directions, I learned that the hotel was within easy walking distance, just up the hill and around the corner from the station. I set off on foot, walked up several hills, got lost, and finally stopped at a posh high-rise apartment building. The doorman, seeing my fatigue and frustration, called a cab for me, and moments later I was in my hotel.

Once I got settled, I made a call to a friend, Phillipe, who lived nearby. I'd met him in Cuba on a humanitarian mission with the Havana Central Pediatric Hospital. Before leaving home I'd emailed him to say I wanted to get together, and now, talking to him on the phone, he invited me to meet him at his restaurant in the small town of Eze, eight kilometers away from Monte Carlo.

I caught a cab and as it pulled up to his place, the restaurant wasn't at all what I'd expected. The neighborhood was run-down and the place itself was a bit shabby. I told myself to relax and have a good time – after all, I could leave whenever I wanted. Phillipe's restaurant reminded me of the paladars, or government-sanctioned eateries, that were so common in Cuba. They often didn't look like much, but the homemade Cuban food and the friendliness of the owners was delightful. So I kept an open mind.

Phillipe descended the wooden stairs with a smile, and my anxiety faded as we hugged and went up to his restaurant. I found my bearings, I allowed a calmness and a quietness to spread inside myself, and my nervous tension disappeared. Phillipe introduced me to his mother, and then he gave me a tour of the restaurant and showed me the brick-fired oven he'd built in the outdoor kitchen. As we walked around looking at the building, which was also his home, he revealed to me his vision of the future and the renovations he planned. His passion for the place and for cooking was obvious as he shared his ideas with me.

We talked about the women in our lives, and he said he'd just returned from visiting his girlfriend in Italy. A short time later we were joined by some others: a husband, wife, and daughters. Phillipe said they were long-time friends of his, and that we'd be the only ones dining on the wooden deck of the restaurant.

That evening I was treated to a feast prepared with a balance of flavors. One of those flavors came from the prickly pear cactus, and I thought, "How amusing! Prickly pear! Here I thought it was unique to the Southwest." Meanwhile, the trip and the events of the previous few days drifted by in my thoughts, and I laid my head back on the wooden railing. Taking in the Mediterranean sea air, I relaxed knowing how in life's simple moments, like this one, our joy of being human fills us with peace.

After dinner, the smoke from fine Cuban cigars filled the air as in the background played the Cuban CD *Reflexion*, and the Corsican music of Charles Marcellesi from *Corsicaboverde*. All my loneliness and longing for home melted into images of my girlfriend relaxing in our warm bed thousands of miles away. I imagined the kiss of her gentle soft lips as I heard the music, smelled the smoke, and peered up to the sky, and I felt as if I were in heaven. To make things even better, after dinner I was treated to a special drink that had been in Phillipe's family for generations; it tasted of ripe fruit surrounded by the warmth of alcohol.

At the end of the evening Phillipe took me back to my hotel. Driving past the yachts and luxurious automobiles of Monte Carlo, I sank into the front seat of his Audi and felt the cool coastal breeze. Finally arriving at my hotel and lying down on my bed, I realized, as my eyes closed, that my exhaustion had melted into a deep sense of peace.

The next morning I felt rested. Before breakfast I went up to the hotel's observation deck for the 360-degree roof-top view of the area. Afterward as I waited for the elevator, I heard a nearby couple speaking in French. Listening in, I realized why French is called a romantic language. The words transcended my language barrier and in that moment, I felt a love beyond knowing.

Downstairs at breakfast I looked at the meats, cheeses, fruits, and breads, and I appreciated the feast in front of me. For some reason I suddenly thought about Itzhak Perlman, one of the world's great violinists. I remembered how, when someone exclaimed, they'd give up their life to play the violin as well as he did, Perlman responded, "I did." In that moment my life and my understanding of it paralleled this in some way. I realized how I had given up life to search, to love God, and ultimately to know myself. This trip, with so little money and so little time, revealed that God is me and that I am God. Through my experiences I receive small precious glimpses into the gift that I am and the gift that each one of us is in the great scheme of things.

Later that evening in my hotel room I wrote the following journal entry:"There is a knowingness that will pass into the heart of love and receptivity. As a new-born babe is cradled in its mother's arms, you gently rest against the beat of Spirit's heart."

I added:

"I no longer wish to say the words . . . I wish to be them."

Such moments of grace reveal my being, and my becoming, and the way life shares her mysteries.

CHAPTER 29

ANTIBES

Antibes in southern France lies on the Mediterranean Sea between Cannes and Nice. The town was founded as a Greek colony in the fifth century BC and named Antipolis, which means "the city across" in ancient Greek. It became a vital center of trade due to its naturally protected harbor.
~ Koshka's Little Travel Guide

After my stay in Monaco I caught a train to Antibes, a lovely town on the French Riviera. I had no hotel reservation, and so upon arrival I strolled down to the ocean and the main part of town before looking for a hotel.

The train trip from Monaco had created an appetite, so I found a harbor-front restaurant with a nice outdoor patio and ordered a salad. I practiced my French on the server – "Je voudrais une salade de Parisian, s'il vous plait" ("I'd like a Parisian salad, please") – and hoped I'd made myself understood and that the kind of salad I wanted would arrive. As I sat waiting, I looked out onto the harbor of small boats with their masts bobbing in the wind. My first impression of Antibes was that it was a lot like the cities in South Florida.

As I awaited for my food, I realized I was on my own in a European town for the first time since my arrival. I was a bit anxious about how I'd get along; I spoke very little French and didn't know any locals who could help me if I got into a predicament. But I relaxed in my chair and enjoyed the aroma of freshly mown grass as, in the distance, a mower trimmed the road's center median. The smell took me back to thoughts of home and of being a young man and tending my own yard. In that moment I felt connected and comforted.

Eventually my food arrived, and I was pleasantly surprised. I'd chosen a "Parisian salad" mostly based on the name, and it was a hearty meal. Nestled with the lettuce and croutons in a large white bowl were two poached eggs, fresh green beans, diced ham, tomatoes, and grilled quartered potatoes. I felt fortunate to have such a hearty lunch, and I thanked the server in my best French: "Merci beaucoup."

I decided to treat myself to desert. I found something on the menu that I thought might be a banana split. I wanted to see how it would compare to the ones back home, so I asked the server about it. As she tried to explain the ingredients and how it was made, a man walked by and said, in English, "She's saying it has whipped cream on top, and she wants to know if you want that." I smiled and said, "Yes, I want that, too!"

The English-speaking man and I talked for a while. He was French and had lived in Austin, Texas, before returning to his homeland. Before he left my table, he gave me some pointers about where to go and what to see while I was there. High on his list of must-see attractions were the Picasso Museum and the Eden Roc resort.

After I'd satisfied my appetite it was time to look for a hotel. I returned to the train station where there was a tourist information booth. Luckily, one of the recommended hotels was very close by.

It was a sparsely furnished place called the Hotel Le Collier, and it cost 100 Euros for one night! This was a lot more than I'd expected to pay for a Spartan room in a small French town. It wasn't even by the beaches. But it was comfortable and clean – a place where I could take a shower and lay my head down to rest at the end of the evening.

After I unpacked my carry-on suitcase, I decided to check out the Picasso Museum. The great painter had visited friends in Antibes in 1923, and he returned as an internationally famous artist after World War II in 1946. During this second visit he remained for six months, which he spent painting and creating ceramics and tapestries. When he left Antibes, Picasso donated many of these artworks to the town, and Antibes established the Picasso Museum.

As I approached the pale tan-colored sandstone building, I saw that it overlooked the turquoise sea. Inside I climbed the stairs to the second floor. In a room on the left I marveled to look through the window at a boat moored in the harbor, and that view through the whitewashed walls was like a painting itself. I stood there for several minutes framing it with my eyes, like a camera, so I would remember its beauty. After that I moved on to viewing the works of the famous artist, many of which I enjoyed immensely. Later I strolled onto the museum's rear veranda, overlooking the sea, and I delighted in the feel of the warm ocean breeze caressing my face.

After several moments of soaking in the breeze, I reentered the building through its wooden door and headed into the gift shop. I labored over which scarf to buy for my girlfriend back home. There were two that I liked: each had one of Picasso's paintings on it. I stood there for a long time wondering which to choose. Back and forth I went before finally making a choice – only to find, on returning to the U.S., that Sarah had a print hanging in our home just like the scarf I'd selected.

My next stop was the Eden Roc resort, or the Hotel du Cap-Eden-Roc, and in the morning after a simple breakfast of hot tea and a croissant, I caught a bus to the southern tip of the tiny cape where it was located. This hotel has been visited by many celebrities, including Marlene Dietrich, Winston Churchill, Charles De Gaulle, Elizabeth Taylor, and Richard Burton. Author F. Scott Fitzgerald used it as the inspiration for the fictional location, the "Hotel des Etrangers," in his novel *Tender Is the Night*, and artist Marc Chagall used one of the beachside cabanas as a tiny studio where he made several sketches. Today it's a favorite haunt of the stars who visit nearby Cannes for the film festival.

I approached the resort in awe of its manicured grounds and buildings. But when I walked out onto the rear veranda I was stunned as this beautiful place revealed its secrets. Exiting the huge French doors I peered out upon acres of beautifully mown grass, lush gardens and trees, and a pool house that framed the magnificent turquoise-colored ocean.

I stood there for quite some time, dreaming of a lifetime in which

I might have lived there, being waited on and fussed over. I envisioned myself playing croquet, riding horses, and feeling silken clothes upon my back. A big smile covered my face. It was just a dream, you know, but sometimes it's fun to dream.

At the pool house I ordered lunch. Afterward I enjoyed a fine Monte Cristo No. 2 Cuban cigar that I'd picked up in a train station. In that moment, while basking in the sun, I felt like a king. This was a place I'd return to when my bank account could afford it. The thought popped into my head of how sometimes my girlfriend Sarah would call me "Lord Fauntleroy" after a 1980s film character, the long-lost son of a wealthy nobleman. She did this because when we traveled I'd occasionally ask for extra services from the hotel staff. Well, here at the Hotel du Cap-Eden-Roc, those additional services wouldn't be so farfetched.

After lunch I strolled along the wide stretch of manicured lawns and through the resort's lobby. I smiled at the concierge who smiled back and said, "Au revoir." Then I headed to the bus stop and back to my reality: the sparsely furnished Le Collier.

As I waited at the bus stop, I took in the views, breathing deeply and feeling a sense of pleasure for being able to experience such a beautiful place. The bus arrived and took me back to the center of town. There I walked among the other tourists, and I stumbled onto an Internet cafe where I could email home. At the computer I experienced the challenge of working a foreign-language keyboard, where the keys are arranged differently than in the U.S. But I let my brain and fingers relax into the newness of the keyboard, and I took great joy in typing and sending an email to my girlfriend back home.

It had been a long day, and soon I returned to the hotel, took a shower, and rested. The next day I would be off to Saint-Raphael and then to Avignon. I didn't know it at the time, but an unexpected trip to Saint-Tropez also lay in store for me.

CHAPTER 30

SAINT - TROPEZ

As I reach for a peach . . . in Saint Tropez . . . I'll gather my far-flung
thoughts together, speeding away on a wind to a new day.
  ~ Roger Waters, Pink Floyd

I arrived in Saint-Raphael at noon on a hot and sticky day. Wiping the sweat from my forehead, I noticed a sign that said Saint-Tropez. The thought of that French Riviera resort town took me back to when I was a young man who loved to get a good summer tan. Bain de Soleil was the suntan lotion to use in those days, and in those moments of spreading that orange gel all over my body, I'd always felt as if I were basking on a beach in southern France. So I decided I just had to visit Saint-Tropez.

I'd originally been headed for Aix-en-Provence, a town known for its history, culture, and museums. It had been frequented by such luminaries as artist Paul Cézanne and writers Emile Zola and Ernest Hemingway. Saint-Tropez, on the other hand, was known as the playground of Brigitte Bardot and, more recently, Beyonce, Kate Moss, and Rihanna.

While I waited at the bus station, my thoughts were churning: Saint-Tropez or Aix-en-Provence? Cézanne and Hemingway or Bardot and Beyonce? Being a red-blooded American male, I decided on Saint-Tropez.

By the time I arrived, the sun was going down soon, so I headed out of the bus station to find a hotel. My first encounter with the locals was with a saleswoman at a very expensive clothing shop. One thing I love doing is looking at beautiful clothes, so I browsed the men's section of the boutique. When I asked the lady if she could recommend a hotel, she snapped at me in her heavy French accent, "Do I look like an information center?" O-kay. I smiled and headed out the door.

I soon learned that because I'd arrived during an international boat show, no rooms were available anywhere in town. To make things worse, I was hungry and most of the restaurants that were open were very expensive. Maybe Beyonce, Kate Moss, and Rihanna could afford them, but I couldn't. Fortunately, I found a small pizza place that I could afford.

As I finished my pepperoni pizza, I decided to sleep on one of the concrete benches at the bus stop. The night was nice and the stars were out in full force so, I thought, "Why not?" As I stretched out on a bench, the last bus of the evening pulled up and the driver asked what I was doing. I replied that no hotel rooms were available, and so I was spending the night right there. I braced myself for the same disdain I'd gotten from the saleswoman in the upscale boutique, but instead, this man looked at me with compassion. He said, "Come with me. I know of a place where you can rent a room for the night."

We drove several miles outside of town, and the night was quite dark as we pulled up to a house surrounded by a stucco and cinder block wall. The driver went inside, and minutes later he emerged followed by an elderly lady. He waived at me to come through the gate, and as I did, I noticed a number of tents scattered around. It was some kind of camping compound. I thanked him, and he told me to wait outside the wall at 5 a.m. the next morning, when the morning bus driver would pick me up and take me back to Saint-Tropez.

I was relieved when the elderly woman led me inside. I knew at least I wouldn't be sleeping on the ground among the tents. But arriving at my room on the second floor, I was assaulted by the strong smell of cat urine. In addition, the door to the next room was open, and I could see a scary-looking guy huddled on his bed in the corner of the room.

I entered my room and locked both doors, the one that led to the hallway and the one that led to the balcony. I spread my towel out on the bed and lay down on it, hoping that nothing would crawl on me in the next few hours as I tried to sleep. I glanced at my watch and saw that it was after midnight.

Exhausted, I closed my eyes and as I was just about to drift off, I was startled by someone yanking on the patio door trying to get into my room. I lay quietly, trying not to make a sound and hoping whoever it was would go away. After that, I didn't get a wink of sleep. By four a.m., I decided to leave the room and wait in the street in the hope that the bus driver might arrive early.

Standing there on the street in the darkness, the memory came to me of a weekend healing conference I'd attended in the basement of someone's house in Rochester, New York. That weekend my girlfriend and I endured the stench of cat urine as we sat on the floor trying to be polite. Later, my girlfriend and I referred to the retreat location as the "Kitty Pee Parlor." Now that I'd had the experience a second time, I wasn't sure which was worse.

Standing there on the tree-lined road in the dark, I watched as one service truck after another rumbled past, presumably headed for the international boat show. Around 5 a.m. at last I saw my bus heading toward me. Boy, was I glad to be leaving!

But as the bus drew closer to me, I realized it wasn't going to stop. Thinking the driver just couldn't see me in the dark, I stepped out into the road and waved my arms back and forth to catch his attention. However, I quickly jumped out of the way as he sped right past me. "Are you kidding?" I exclaimed. In my frustration I let out a primal scream that I'm sure woke up the neighborhood.

I decided to hitchhike into town, so I stuck out my thumb. Minutes later a young man in a little old beater of a car pulled over. I sighed with relief and said in my best French that I wanted to go to the bus station in Saint-Tropez. He smiled, nodded, and off we went.

A short time later I was finally at the Saint-Tropez bus station where I bought a ticket on the next bus out of town. During the time before my bus arrived, I walked around town and found a small coffee shop. I ate a couple of croissants and sipped a cup of Earl Grey tea. "It's great to be back in civilization," I thought, remembering the cat pee hotel with a shudder. Later, waiting for the bus at the station, I wrote the following in my leather-bound journal: "There certainly are a lot of smokers in France. Wish I had gone to Aix-en-Provence. Sitting on a concrete bench I smell my soap and toiletries on my skin, and I feel comforted. I realize that my spiritual quest is to love those around me, Sarah, and myself. . . ."

By now it was now 7:30 a.m. and I was back on the bus. Thank God! During the bus ride back to Saint-Raphael, I reflected on my journey, asking myself, "How is this trip like my life?" I realized that much of the trip was built on a frenetic energy, running from place to place. And I'd had moments of bliss, as well. Looking out at the sea through the bus windows I concluded that this trip was truly another reminder of my life. For most of my life I'd been running to the next experience, sometimes forgetting to slow down and enjoy the experience itself. I realized my life was ruled by the personas I'd created for myself to stay emotionally safe and to conform with what I thought society wanted from me.

As I sat with these thoughts I looked back upon the events of the trip so far in Germany, Monaco, Antibes, and even in the Kitty Pee Parlor of Saint-Tropez. Each event revealed that both the internal and external journeys had resonated with something deep inside me. I re- laxed into the seat and recognized the judgments inside my head as I watched people get on and off the bus. Some were fat, some were skinny, some were pretty, some were ugly. And some moved too slowly. My judgments of others swirled inside my brain. And then I noticed my judgments of myself: about not being enough, about moving too quickly, and then about moving too slowly. All of the thoughts were reflected back to me from the outside world.

I took a deep breath, and that brought me back into myself and to the understanding that this was my journey and no one else's. In that moment I slowed my mind, took several more deep breaths, and gazed through the bus window out over the beautiful Mediterranean Sea. I felt thankful that I was learning about myself and that I'd had the courage and strength to take this journey.

CHAPTER 31

Avignon

Sur le pont d'Avignon / L'on y danse, l'on y danse.
Sur le pont d'Avignon / L'on y danse tous en rond.
Translation:
On the bridge of Avignon / We all dance there, we all dance there.
On the bridge of Avignon / We all dance there in a ring.
   ~ Fifteenth-Century French Song

I took the famous TGV ("train a grande vitesse" or high-speed train) and traveled like lightning to Avignon. It was one of the oldest towns in France, dating from pre-Roman times. Later it was home to the popes of the Catholic Church who lived in the splendid Papal Palace near the center of town.

Arriving in Avignon I stepped down from the train and into the sunlight. I sensed that this was a very different place than any I'd seen so far on my trip. I felt a peaceful lightness in the air, and unlike Saint-Tropez, this place seemed to welcome me.

I caught a local bus to the center of the town, and as we passed through Avignon's ancient stone walls, I felt as if I were traveling back in time. I also had a sense of coming home again. Relaxed yet excited, I exited the bus. I strolled around town for a while, enjoying the scenery and architecture and finally ending up at the visitor information center where I was greeted by a friendly and enthusiastic young man. He recommended the reasonably priced Hotel de L'Horloge (in English, "The Clock Hotel") a few blocks away. So far Avignon was a pleasant surprise and a welcome change from Saint-Tropez. And the town held many more surprises. I easily found the hotel, and on the way I passed a street sign for the Rue de la Balance. "How appropriate," I thought.

My room at the Hotel de L'Horloge was nicely appointed and very comfortable, and as I unpacked, I encountered another surprise. Before I had left on this trip, Sarah had put a greeting card in my luggage with instructions not to open it until this day. I pulled the card from my bag's zippered compartment, and as I opened the envelope I felt happily connected to her. But as I glanced at the picture on the outside of the card, my feelings turned to a subtle anxiety. The card depicted a knight in shining armor embracing a young woman. On the inside, the words said that I was to lead the way for the two of us.

I grappled with the idea of trying to lead the way, whether it was along the new career path of counseling that we both had chosen or whether we should each be on our own for a while. I'd been struggling to determine what I was supposed to do, both employment-wise and in my relationship. There was an enormous pressure on me: the weight of not knowing whether I could, indeed, "lead the way." Part of me wanted to snap my fingers and make everything okay for the both of us, yet another part knew I was struggling with my own life and its direction. And all of this intensified the reality that I didn't have a job waiting when I got home.

Meanwhile my money was running low, and this added to my anxiety, even though after Avignon I'd be volunteering at Lourdes and so would have inexpensive accommodations, and after that I'd be visiting some friends of a friend at their country home. I reminded myself that this trip was about my own exploration, so I came back into the moment. I knew I should check my email, so I calmed myself and headed for the hotel's computer room. There I emailed Sarah, telling her how I missed her. I added that I loved her and looked forward to seeing her again. Then I signed off and headed into the streets of Avignon.

As I exited the hotel, again I saw the street sign for the Rue de la Balance. I walked up and down the center of town and through the many side streets looking into shop windows. The little stores held many treasures, but the thing that impressed me most was the people. Everyone seemed so happy!

There was a museum I wanted to visit called the Calvet Museum. It wasn't far from my hotel, but as I walked around looking for it, I got lost. I asked directions a few times, but the directions conflicted with each other, so I got even more lost. Rather than being upset, however, I smiled as I wandered along, thinking about how life was like this, getting misdirected and lost, and about how if you want to find the right path you have to do it yourself.

Finally I arrived at the museum, and as I entered the portico, it seemed incredibly familiar. The museum was housed in an eighteenth-century mansion, and as I walked through it, I was struck by this sense of familiarity several times. On the first floor I stood for several minutes admiring the sculpture of a reclining woman. As my eyes moved along her body's contours, tears rolled down my cheeks. I felt almost as though I were making love with her, and I was transported to another century. I must have looked upset, for I was abruptly brought back into the moment by a security guard asking me if everything was okay. I smiled at her and said, "Yes."

The more I explored the museum, the more familiar this mansion seemed. Holding the iron handrail of the steps leading to the second floor, I felt as though I were heading to my own private study and bed-room. The huge chandelier and the frescoed walls seemed to welcome me back, and I paused to let these feelings soak in.

I snapped several photos of the beautiful Egyptian-themed paintings with their lovely female subjects, vibrant colors, and painted textures. The brush strokes and varnish on the canvas seemed to have a life of their own. Once again I was brought back into the moment when a young French mother and her beautiful daughter peered around the corner at me, giggling. I felt as though I were a child myself, and as I blushed they vanished as quickly as they'd appeared. Then I felt a longing to hold my girlfriend who was so many miles away. Finally leaving the museum, I turned several times to gaze back at the huge stone walls and gate, and then I rounded the corner and the mansion was out of my sight.

My next stop was the Papal Palace. I strolled through the small monastic rooms used by the monks for sleeping, and I explored the grounds. I also visited the massive receiving parlors, and I felt mixed of emotions. The strength and the grandeur contained in those walls was obvious to me, yet I also felt a sense of repression and control. The stonework and hand-hewn beams gave me a sense of history and the feeling that mankind has been on earth for many generations and will be here for many more to come. I became deeply aware of the continuity of life, and confident that my own life would continue in many more places and over many more lifetimes. Meanwhile I felt deep within myself that I had once walked within these large stone rooms.

It was getting late, the museums were closing, and I was famished from all of the walking and sightseeing. I decided to head north through the streets to explore the rest of the town and find a restaurant. Again I got lost, so I asked a policeman for directions and was embarrassed when he pointed out that I'd had the map upside down the whole time!

I finally found a nice place to eat within view of the tower of the Papal Palace. A young couple from England were dining at a nearby table, and we struck up a conversation. We discussed our religious and spiritual beliefs, and our travels in France and the United States.

That conversation was the perfect end to a perfect day, and that night I enjoyed a peaceful sleep.

CHAPTER 32

LOURDES

I do not at all understand the mystery of grace — only that it meets us where we are but does not leave us where it found us.
   ~ Anne Lamott

From Avignon, I caught the train to Lourdes.
   Before I continue, let me explain the significance of this holy place. In 1858, a fourteen-year-old peasant girl named Bernadette had a vision of the Virgin Mary in a small cave or grotto outside what was then the small country town of Lourdes. Since then, the town has become a leading Roman Catholic shrine with 200 million visitors since 1860. The water that flows from the spring in the grotto is believed to have healing properties, and the Catholic church has officially recognized sixty-eight miraculous healings. Numerous other cures have taken place at Lourdes for which there is no physical or psychological basis beyond the healing power of the water.

   Before leaving the U.S., I had arranged to do volunteer work at Lourdes. Nevertheless, after arriving there at the train station, I was confused about where the grotto was and how to get there. Fortunately outside the train station I found the right bus and arrived at the hospitality center for the shrine.

   The man behind the counter didn't speak English, and in my very rudimentary French I tried to explain that I was there to do volunteer work and that I needed a room for the night: *Je voudrais une chamber* pour le soir. He responded politely in French, but he spoke so quickly that I couldn't make out a single word. I just stood there with a wide-eyed look, not knowing what to do next.

An American, a tour leader named Claire, came to my rescue, and she helped me get settled. I gathered my meal tickets, map, and key, we exited the office, and she pointed me toward the north gate. On the way to my dorm, I walked past many shops selling religious gifts and memorabilia for tourists and those in need of healing.

At the dormitory, I entered the security code, which was 9-1-1. I realized that the date was September 11, and I had a sudden feeling that something remarkable would happen during my stay. I asked Spirit to please deliver the event, whatever it would be, in such a way that I could deal with it with ease and grace. I unpacked quickly and headed back to the shops.

The first place I entered was just across the street. The shop contained so many rosaries, candles, and vestments that I could have started my own church. One rosary caught my eye. It wasn't anything fancy, just a simple rosewood item dotted with a bit of silver. I picked it up several times but decided not to purchase it – I had to conserve my money. I put it back on the shelf with the odd feeling that it would show up again somehow during my trip. Leaving the shop without buying anything, I entered through, St Michael's gate to the gathering area outside the cathedral.

Preparations were underway for the internationally famous torchlight procession. One processioner carried an eight-foot chrome cross. Four pilgrims bore a huge statue of the Virgin Mary enclosed with glass panels in a housing of ebony. My heart sped with excitement as I watched the preparations – this was one of the reasons for my trip, and it was actually happening!

An invigorating chill was in the air as we made our way across the bridge over the river. Loudspeakers announced that the procession would soon begin. As pilgrims filled their glass and plastic containers with water from the grotto, I decided I would take some home for myself and my friends. Looking up toward Lourdes Cathedral as I filled my container with holy water, I saw the glistening lights of hundreds of candles carried by the pilgrims.

As the procession advanced, I was awestruck by the many twinkling candles. It was the kind of experience you want to share with someone you love. Tears filled my eyes as I looked around to see if my beloved was somehow magically there with me. Realizing that she wasn't, my heart ached and my thoughts flew to her. I felt as though I were missing a part of myself because she wasn't with me.

The procession continued, with prayers said in a multitude of languages. The intensity and scope of the event was extremely moving. We crossed the cathedral grounds, and I felt an overwhelming admiration for the faithful and hopeful people in attendance. Sick people, families, children, the aged, individuals, and groups all prayed for a miraculous healing. It was an event I'd remember for the rest of my life.

The next morning I headed back to the hospitality center where I met with Father Paul, a Canadian priest. When I saw the rosary he held in his hands, I was pleasantly surprised: it was nearly identical to the rosewood item that had attracted my attention in the gift shop the previous night. This was a very good omen, as if Spirit or the angels were assuring me I was in the right place and was connected to them. Strong emotions welled up, and I remembered how, some time earlier at Unity Village in Kansas City, I'd resisted my feelings and refused to allow my heart to open. Now I said in a silent prayer that I was open to Mary, to Saint Bernadette (the peasant girl who'd had the vision at the grotto), and to the light of Christ. In response, I heard a voice in my head say, "Face the fear of your own being-ness, your own vulnerability."

Father Paul shared the history of Bernadette with myself and the other members of the orientation group. He mentioned that when Bernadette was visited in the grotto by the Virgin Mary, she'd resisted opening her heart to the apparitions. I was enormously comforted by hearing this, and it eased some of my regrets about not opening up at Unity Village.

Father Paul assigned me to go to the train station and help the infirm descend from the train. He explained that this would consist of helping them walk to the wheelchairs that awaited them. I'd also help with those who arrived lying down on gurneys.

When we broke for lunch, I spent some time with Claire, our group leader, and Carolyn, who'd been a novice but had chosen not to take her vows as a nun. On learning that my name was Kevin, they told me about Kevin of Glendalough, a wealthy Irish nobleman who renounced worldly goods, became an ascetic priest, founded an important monastery in Ireland, and was eventually recognized as a saint. Each Catholic saint is assigned a day on which he or she is honored, called a "feast day," and Saint Kevin's feast day was June third – Saint Bernadette's birthday. On hearing this, I smiled and felt a surge of happiness.

After lunch I was off to receive my instructions at the train station. The facilitators spent several hours explaining the various types of wheelchairs, gurneys, and other devices, and how to use them. The next morning there was more training: Claire and Father Paul gave us information about helping others and about learning our way around the grounds. The day flew by.

Meanwhile, I felt exhausted. In addition to the rigorous training and the emotional intensity of being at such a holy place, one of my roommates in the dorm snored like a freight train. So I'd gotten little sleep since my arrival in Lourdes. Now, as the procession was beginning once again, I felt as if all of my nerve endings were frayed.

But I had responsibilities. I'd been designated to help forty other people hold a rope around an area in front of the cathedral as a means of crowd control. This was done to make sure no one would be injured or crushed by the throngs in the procession. As I stood waiting for the rope to arrive, I felt faint. My vision went blurry, and suddenly I could barely stay on my feet. As I wobbled back and forth, nearly slipping into an unconscious state, I fervently prayed to Mother Mary to help me stand and complete my task for the evening. My lightheadedness got so bad that at one point I had to drop to one knee. Embarrassed, I tried to make it look as though I were genuflecting. I prayed, "Mary, please help me stand, give me strength and I will do your work," chanting my plea over and over in my mind.

All of a sudden my team leader, an elderly gentleman from England, called out to me to come with him into the vestibule where the sacred glass and ebony carriage of Mary's huge statue and the enormous chrome cross were stored. His voice infused me with new energy, and I felt a tangible shift in consciousness. I really wanted to help this man, and I was suddenly clear headed, alert, and grounded – my prayers had been answered.

We climbed the stairs and entered the church. The Englishman asked me to carry the eight-foot shining chrome cross out into the courtyard for the procession. What an honor it was to hold this sacred item! I picked it up and was refreshed by the coolness of the chrome against my feverish face. Glancing upward, I sent deep gratitude to Mary for hearing my prayers and helping me regain full consciousness. With a new jolt of energy from the sensation of the cool chrome on my skin, I carried the cross onto the front steps of the basilica. Moments later I was asked to pass it to the woman who'd been selected to carry it for the procession, and I was filled with enthusiasm to have carried the cross for even those few moments. The experience took me back to many happy memories of being an altar boy in grade school.

I shuffled back to my position to hold the rope for the masses of people who would soon arrive. The weakness returned, and I struggled the whole evening to stay fully conscious while holding the rope. As the procession ended, I felt strangely angry that I hadn't been able to help more people because I myself had been feeling sick. At the same time, I felt a sense of resentment that no one had ministered to me for my illness, while everyone else was being cared for. It was an odd revelation: I was aware that I was judging others who were ill, while I, too, was ill and was angry with myself about it. Perhaps it was a lesson in empathy and compassion, and I had to get angry to understand it.

Meanwhile, all I could think was that I needed to lie down. I trudged through the crowds, worried that I wouldn't make it back to my room. Traveling alone comes with risks that you never consider when you're excited about a trip. The fear snowballed: What if I needed a physician? How would I communicate with a doctor? How would I pay for medical care? I was hyperventilating as I walked the few blocks back to my dorm, where I collapsed on my bed. I heard my dorm mate snoring, and again I didn't get the sleep I needed.

The morning came much too quickly. By now I was in a state of self-pity that flowed as steadily as the holy water from the Lourdes grotto. I still felt angry, and now I was also unsettled and disappointed that I didn't feel at peace.

My thoughts turned to Father Paul's rosary, and I decided it and my illness together were a sign that I should make a confession with him and explain what was happening in my life. So I did. It had been twenty-five years since my last confession, and it was comforting to be speaking privately to a priest once again. I shared with Father Paul how I just didn't seem able to get my life back on track since losing my business and my home in the economic downturn. I also spoke of the struggles in my relationship and about my financial situation, and how all of this was causing my shortness of temper.

He listened attentively, and then he said, "Don't you think it is time to stop crawling and to stand on your own two feet?" He recommended that I move into my own place, even if it was a tiny closet, and that I take care of myself and no one else. Tears welled up in my eyes as he spoke to me.

His final words to me were these: "In suffering, if there is love, true growth occurs to a new level of compassion and awareness."

After my confession I headed into town, and as I walked, I was secure in the knowledge that he had spoken the truth. I did need to be on my own so I could feel more grounded and self-sufficient. I found a computer and emailed Sarah, saying that I loved her and that I needed some time for myself, so when I returned I would move out. I clicked the "send" button and returned to my room.

As mentioned earlier, before leaving the U.S. I'd completed a ten-day intensive practicum for my master's degree in spiritual psychology, and one of the things I'd been told at the end of that program was not to make any major life decisions for the next 30 days. It was now only two weeks since I'd received this advice, and again I'd gone against it.

As dawn broke, I left the dorm and went to the American Red Cross for help. I didn't know what was wrong with me, but I could still barely walk and I knew I was in trouble, health-wise. I waited in the cold for the Red Cross to open, and I was relieved when the nurse finally arrived to open the door. She and another nurse examined me, taking my temperature having me say "ah" with a tongue depressor in my mouth. I was too sick to follow what they were saying, but when one of them said, "Doctor," I was incredibly grateful and relieved.

I was treated for severe dehydration and a urinary tract infection. The doctor gave me antibiotics told me to return to my room for a few days of recuperation. I was told in no uncertain terms to stay in bed. All that day and evening, I slept and rehydrated myself with fluids. I drank so much water and cranberry juice that by that evening the extreme pain I had felt all over my body was letting up.

I awoke at 4 a.m. to laughter and tears. These were tears of joy and surrender. I was laughing and crying with joy at the same time!

The thing that had awakened me was a song that I had heard before but that had carried little significance for me. It was "Blackbird" by the Beatles. The lyrics speak of broken wings, of learning to fly, and of gaining freedom.

In my laughter and tears I felt my shoulders pop as though something had realigned my shoulder blades. And suddenly, the pain was gone. I continued laughing and crying tears of joy and gratitude for quite some time as the words of the song continued, revealing a moment of grace.

The next morning I was able to rejoin the volunteers in my group. With Albert, my group leader, and several other men, we walked the Stations of the Cross, starting and ending behind the beautiful church. I felt a closeness with these men as each of us read passages of the stations from a spiritual pamphlet.

I suddenly realized that all my anger about myself and the sick people was gone. I had a new lease on life, and I was filled with gratitude. With my newfound feeling of health and thankfulness, I would soon leave Lourdes on the next leg of my journey, to visit some friends of a friend in the French countryside. Because of the extra time spent recuperating, I'd have fewer days in Paris, but that was okay. I accepted that everything happens for a reason, and that this applied in my current situation.

I'd learned about forgiveness and acceptance. As I enjoyed my final meal in Lourdes, I was overwhelmingly thankful that my health was restored. Exiting the restaurant, I glanced up at the walnut trees lining the river. I saw five vibrant new leaves blowing in the wind directly above my head. This was unusual because it was autumn and none of the other trees had any green on them. With joy and amazement I stared at the leaves on the branches six feet above my head, and for me they were a sign of renewal and new growth, and an affirmation that life endures, continuing season after season, experience after experience.

CHAPTER 33

A FRENCH MILL HOUSE

I love making new friends, and I respect people for a lot of different reasons
   ~ Taylor Swift

On the train bound for my next destination – Gueret, France – I sat next to a couple from Kansas and another couple from Florida. It was a relief to talk to them and hear English spoken, a relief from the strain of trying to communicate in a foreign language. We chatted about our loved ones and our travels, and before I knew it, we were approaching the station at Gueret.

In Gueret I planned to visit Heinrich and Ella, the friends of a friend. I'd never met them, and I was a little anxious about meeting new people and not knowing what they'd be like. My friend back home said Heinrich had been a photographer in the 1990s for national magazines such as *Vanity Fair* and *Vogue*, and that he'd done photo shoots of famous musicians, as well. He was a perfectionist at times, my friend said, and if he didn't like you things could become uncomfortable. I was intrigued as we pulled into the station.

Getting off the train, I was approached by a large, tall, blond man with a German accent. We shook hands and sat down for a beer. Our conversation flowed effortlessly as we talked about our lives.

He shared the story of how he'd gotten to where he was, and I shared how I was struggling to figure out what to do next. We left the station, and as we drove through the French countryside to his home, we discussed my unemployment and my relationship. He recommended that I find a small room of my own, get back on my feet, put money in my pocket, and put the relationship on hold. This was remarkably similar to what Father Paul had suggested a day earlier.

Heinrich lived in La Celle-Dunoise in Limousin in central France. It was a tiny village adorned by an ancient and picturesque bridge across the Creuse River. There was also the Church of Saint Pierre, which dated back to the twelfth century.

La Celle-Dunoise was only twelve kilometers from Gueret, so we soon arrived at Heinrich's home. There I met his wife Ella, a cheerful and petite brunette. They lived in a restored French mill house, the Moulin de Sardiex, and entering it was like walking into a dream.

I'd envisioned staying in such a place for much of my life. It was a spacious, light, and airy stone structure with large French doors. Nearby, a flowing stream filled the air with its sounds as the water flowed over a waterfall. Ivy and flowering vines climbed the exterior walls. I felt right at home, and Heinrich and Ella invited me to stay as long as I liked. That was tempting, but I knew I'd be there only for a few days.

What a wonderful chef Ella was! Everything she served was teeming with the rich ingredients of the area: produce, bread, fish, meats, and lots of butter and cream. That evening's meal – salmon, fresh vegetables, and much more – was a feast. After dinner Heinrich, Ella, and I talked into the wee hours. I felt blessed to be there.

The next day as we ate breakfast, Heinrich said he needed to stack some cords of wood that were outside his stone shed. I was delighted to be able to help. The manual labor of that day helped me get grounded. I restacked the two cords already in the shed, and moved the two new cords inside. After the morning's work, Heinrich showed me his prized possession, housed safely behind two huge barn doors: a 1965 Citroen. So French and so cool! I was in awe.

For lunch Ella served her version of the Parisian salad that I'd loved in Antibes. We lunched outside, and I marveled at the peace and joy of my surroundings. A row of trees caught my attention. A dozen of them stood arranged in two perfect rows. I imagined archers standing at one end and practicing their skill by aiming arrows at a target some fifty feet away. After lunch I enjoyed a Cuban Montecristo Edmundo cigar, and in that moment I couldn't imagine being anywhere else in the world but where I was.

That afternoon I did some yard work and pruned the trees. Heinrich and I talked about another mill house in the next county that he wanted to restore. He was so impressed with my energy and skills and diligence that he suggested I work for him and restore it. He offered to feed me and let me live on the property while I did the restoration. But it was an immense project; for example, the structure barely had a roof. He was kind to make the offer, but I needed to earn money, so I thanked him but declined, and we both smiled.

Meanwhile, staying in a place like Heinrich and Ella's mill house fulfilled a dream I'd had for many years. And better still was their hospitality, their kind natures, and the great food Ella prepared. I was sad to leave, but I had somewhere else to go – Chartres Cathedral, another long-awaited destination – so our visit ended a few mornings later.

I waved to Ella as Heinrich and I drove away down the gravel drive. During the short ride to the station in Gueret, I knew I'd made two friends for life. I felt privileged to have met them.

196

CHAPTER 34

CHARTRES CATHEDRAL

I never weary of great churches. . . . Mankind was never so happily inspired as when it made a cathedral.
  ~ Robert Louis Stevenson

Almost since childhood, I'd been intrigued by the great cathedral at Chartres. Construction on what in French is called the "Cathedrale Notre-Dame de Chartres" began in 1205 and lasted 66 years. The result is considered the most magnificent Gothic cathedral in France, and one of the finest cathedrals in the world. For this reason it's included on the United Nations' list of World Heritage Sites or places of outstanding cultural importance to our common heritage as human beings.

So from Gueret I caught the train to Chartres. During the trip I immersed myself in reading about the spiritual dimension of the healing arts. As I read the material I made notes in the margins, and integrated the information in my mind with what I'd learned during my last two years studying spiritual psychology. I was quite content thinking about the healing work I'd be able to do in workshops and seminars to help others.

I was nearing the end of my travels, and as I descended from the train in Chartres, I felt both exhausted and excited by the overall trip and the diversity of places I'd explored. Walking into town I reflected on each stop I'd made along the way and how each place had revealed something challenging, profound, or insightful, and had produced some kind of deeper understanding about myself. I had no reason to expect that my exploration of Chartres would be any different.

Approaching the great cathedral, I was utterly disappointed to see that most of its beautiful façade was covered in scaffolding. A full-blown restoration was taking place both outside and inside the church. Although the scaffolding marred my view, I tried to feel pleased that the cathedral was being restored and maintained for future generations.

The nearby Maison Saint Yves, a seventeenth-century building that was once a seminary, had been highly recommended to me by a female friend who'd once been the interpreter for a Catholic bishop. A few years ago the Maison had been restored as quarters for those, such as myself, making the pilgrimage to Chartres Cathedral. At the reception desk, the view from the window revealed a row of trees neatly lining the courtyard. The courtyard and trees were just like the ones I'd often seen in magazine photos of various places in France, and the sight of them cheered me – until the concierge told me no rooms were available.

An annual festival of lights was taking place that weekend. I soon learned that not only were no rooms available at the Maison Saint Yves, there wasn't a single room to be had anywhere in town. I was really annoyed at myself because the friend who'd recommended the Maison had warned me that I might need an advance reservation because it is usually pretty busy. Ignoring her suggestion, I'd tried to wing it, thinking I'd reserve the room upon arrival. Now my mind was full of judgments about myself for not heeding her advice.

Amid this self-directed negativity, I felt compelled to gain some sense of home and to ground myself in the midst of the confusion. I decided to send an email to Sarah back in the U.S. My last communication with her had been the email from Lourdes about my need to move out and to put our relationship on hold until I got back on my feet. I was concerned to know how she had taken the message and what she'd been thinking and doing since receiving it. Many thoughts about Sarah and our relationship flooded my mind: Was I making a mistake? Did I really need to leave our house? I knew that I loved her with all my heart, but I felt scared and confused about our relationship.

I spent the next hour or so waiting to get onto the single computer that was available for visitors at the crowded Maison Saint Yves. To make things worse, the computer had an outdated and sluggish dial-up connection that took forever to work. This didn't help my mood, and I continued to blame myself for every aspect of my situation. Seeking some mental and spiritual relief, I decided to go into the cathedral. So luggage in hand, I passed through the huge doorway of the great Chartres Cathedral, hoping for some sense of peace inside the walls.

As I walked through the immense and ornate doors and across the threshold, I scanned the cathedral's interior and the large labyrinth that lay before me. Again, the scaffolding obscured my view, lining most of the walls. My spirits sunk even deeper. I had waited for so many years to see the magnificent interior of Chartres Cathedral, and here it was, covered with scaffolding and a huge cloth that hung down to the ground. In that moment the only bright spot in my mood was that before leaving home, I'd watched a video showing the interior in detail, including the historically significant stone carvings that I was now unable to see.

Meanwhile, as I stood on the ancient threshold, I heard Spirit tell me to be quiet. And to take time for myself. So I sat down and began to pray.

As I prayed, I understood that this trip was a reflection of my own life, frenetic and unknown. It was if the trip was reflecting back to me how my mind processed my life. I came to understand that this fast-paced trip was indicative of how I needed peace and stability in my life. Since my crisis in the walk-in humidor at my shop, and my experience of being in the light, and the depression that had followed, I hadn't yet discovered how to put my feet back on the ground. I just didn't know how to live in this world. And now this trip was reminding me once again that home was several thousand miles away and that, as much as I wanted my life to go back to the way it was when I was happily running my tobacco shop, those days were gone forever. Things had changed, and something inside of me was also changing.

Back outside the cathedral, it had grown dark and a drizzling rain was falling. With no place to stay that evening and seeking to get out of the weather, I crossed the street and entered a restaurant. I sat down next to a window and ordered what would probably be one of my last restaurant meals, as my funds were nearly exhausted. There was that evening and one more before I returned home to Sedona, and I hoped my money would somehow last.

As I dined I reflected even more deeply on my present situation. My mind seemed to be unraveling, and it was filled with thoughts of just walking into the streets of Paris and never coming out. My sense of despair grew until an older woman, an American sitting nearby with her husband, suddenly turned to me and asked what was I was doing and why was I there at Chartres.

I looked at her and was stunned to see that she strongly resembled a counselor from whom I'd sought advice many times in Sedona. On some level, I'd always viewed this counselor as the loving mother that I'd never had. So at that moment, I opened up the floodgates of my thoughts and emotions to this woman, a total stranger.

I shared what my life had been like up to that moment. I told her about my being in the light, about losing all my worldly belongings, and about the many experiences I'd had in the past days as I'd traveled through France. I also shared my confusion about my relationship, how I loved my girlfriend but couldn't seem to find any sense of groundedness in my life. Moreover, I told her of the anger inside me, and how I wanted more than anything to find out its origin and to release it. Finally, I shared with her that this trip was about me trying to find myself.

Then a strange thing happened. After I told her of the unbearable fear that I'd felt and that I was feeling in that moment, she opened up to me and told me her own life story and why she and her husband had come to Chartres.

As she spoke, her voice comforted me. My anxieties subsided as I listened to her with empathy. She shared her own periods of living hell, and how God had always helped her through to the next stage of her life. She revealed that she and her husband were on this trip because she'd realized how she had put their marriage on the back burner. She shared her realizations of how their love was more important than anything else. I could recognize the truth of what she was saying by her facial expressions and by the way her eyes sparkled as she said the words. Her husband nodded with a smile that filled my heart.

I felt the unconditional love of a mother who listened and shared her life with me. The experience was yet another powerful affirmation that when we most need an angel to enter our lives, the angel will appear bringing reassurance and hope. Perhaps coincidentally – or perhaps not! – I learned that she, too, like my spiritual mother and counselor, had been a minister in a Religious Science church.

When our conversations came to an end, she and her husband both hugged me. I felt at peace inside. A sense of calm settled once more, and I said to myself, as I'd said before, "I no longer want to speak the words, but I want to be them." And this time I added, "With a little more ease and grace, please."

God once more had brought the gift of exactly the right person into my life at precisely the right moment, so that I could take the next step that I needed to take.

In my newfound calmness, I decided to reward myself for having the courage to take this inner soul journey. And I needed to take care of my inner child. So after leaving the restaurant I entered the pastry shop next door and ordered a delicious chocolate éclair. But as I noticed that there were no available chairs, I cancelled the order. The waitress looked at me and said in French, "Wait one moment." She went outside and seconds later she returned with a chair in her hand and placed it next to her counter. She wiped it dry and gestured for me to sit down, and this thought entered my mind: "Thank you, God, for you have sent yet another angel to help me."

I sat there for what seemed like an hour, warm and dry as the rain poured outside. And I wrote in my journal an entry that described this trip and my life up to this point. I ended the entry with these words: "I feel like I am being pulled through the eye of a needle."

I remembered how I had almost cancelled the trip when I'd noticed that I'd left my passport at home. Deep within myself I knew that I would not have understood my life had I not spent these last few days in France. My previous thought of going into the streets of Paris and never coming out returned briefly. But it dissipated as the greater part of me knew that even though my life would never be the same, I would weather this storm and any others that might come my way – just as the great Cathedral at Chartres would weather the pouring rain tonight as it had done so well since it had been built hundreds of years ago.

With these thoughts in my mind, I closed my journal and headed out into the rain falling on the world's most beautiful cathedral to find a resting place for the night.

CHAPTER 35

PARIS, AU REVOIR

A walk about Paris will provide lessons in history, in beauty, and in the point of Life.
  ~ Thomas Jefferson

I finally arrived in Paris in the evening, tired and weary and nearly penniless. Emerging from the train station, I crossed the street to a cafe where I had a simple sandwich and some water. As I watched the Parisians pass by the window, I wondered what my night would be like when the restaurant closed.

I soon found out as I recrossed the street to the train station and sat on the cold damp ground outside its locked doors. I sensed that I'd leave this city of my dreams the way I'd first come to it: pacing outside another train station in the cold and drizzling rain. Eventually I lay down on the pavement with some "clochards" or French homeless men. I watched them wrap themselves in bubble wrap and plastic to keep out the dampness and the cold, and I realized that although this was their life, soon I'd be headed home and this moment would pass. Spirit had, it seemed, one more lesson for me.

Lacking any plastic of my own, I was crouched on the pavement shivering and trying to keep warm when a fight broke out between two of the homeless men. They were young and very angry, and they screamed at each other in French. Because I was huddled against a concrete wall, it was impossible for me to move away from them,

206

and I cringed, concerned that any moment one of them would either fall on me or drag me into their fight, or both.

Instead their anger stopped almost as quickly as it had begun.

My heart was still pounding with fear when suddenly I saw anger in a new way. I was aware of the little boy inside me who was often trembling with fright. I also realized what anger looked like from the perspective of the recipient or someone defenseless against it. I'd been shaken up by the experience with the two homeless men, and now I knew what it must be like for others when I expressed my own anger. I felt a deep sympathy for my loved ones, especially Sarah, whom I loved so deeply and who waited for me at home.

I remembered all the times she'd helped me – from bridging loans so I could complete my master's degree, to finding a place for me to live while I was going through depression after my dark night of the soul. I also recalled her gift that had enabled me to come on this trip. In that moment I wished I could have told her how, because of my financial vulnerability, I'd placed a wall of anger between us. I then realized that this was a pattern both my father and mother shared.

After the fight between the homeless men subsided, I was unable to sleep. And so at 2 a.m. I found myself there on the pavement scribbling in my journal. I began writing a letter to Sarah that explained everything I had just realized and had previously been unable to express. I told how much her love meant to me. The fight had shown me the hurt I must have inflicted upon her. I wrote a few final words: "I love you with all of my heart and soul." As I closed my journal I felt my heart open wider, and I held her there in my thoughts.

Finally the station doors opened. It was 6:30 a.m., but the city was still covered in darkness. I took the Metro to the Eiffel Tower, where I stood underneath it staring up into the structure. It gave me a haunted feeling, looking into the large skeleton of iron girders traveling upward toward a small light above. Sorrow came over me because Sarah wasn't there to share that moment with me; a sadness filled my heart because I wasn't holding her hand as I gazed upward.

Nearby was a large grassy area lined with trees. I lingered there a while, then I crossed the river – the Seine – and just gazed upon the city. Knowing I'd see these sights again one day, I thought of how wonderful it would be to lounge on the patio of a French Bohemian bistro listening to colorfully dressed artists and intellectuals debate in multiple languages. But that would have to happen at another time, I thought, as I descended into the Metro once again to catch the subway train to the Louvre.

The Louvre was massive. Outside, hordes of tourists from around the world stood in a long line waiting to enter. I was excited to be there, but after another in a series of sleepless nights, I felt a fatigue that permeated the core of my being. I might as well have been thousands of miles away as I strolled through the halls of elegant sculptures and famous paintings. I was still longing for my girlfriend, and I felt deeply alone.

It now seems like a dream when I remember entering the room that housed the Mona Lisa. People by the hundreds were photographing, and for me, the swarms of tourists drained the life from the artist's subject. It was ironic: in my loneliness I was surrounded by crowds of people, and their presence was rather annoying. I'd much rather have been able to contemplate the artwork in private.

Nevertheless, I managed to find some rooms of paintings that spoke to my heart. They were paintings of lovers embracing. I stood for some time, entranced by them.

Several hours later, now fully exhausted, I made my final subway ride to Charles de Gaulle Airport for my fourteen-hour trip back home. As I boarded the plane I blew Paris a kiss.
I whispered, "Au revoir, mon amour."

CHAPTER 36

LANDSCAPING

*Travel is more than the seeing of sights; it is a change that goes on, deep
and permanent, in the ideas of living.*
  ~ Miriam Beard

I knew that I'd returned from France a changed man, and I was soon
to find out how changed I really was.

But first, I had to get a job – and fast! I was nearly broke, I'd soon be
living on my own, and I wasn't even sure what kind of job to look
for. So I updated my resume and searched the want ads. I was willing
to do whatever work I could find. At heart, however, I was still an
entrepreneur, and working for others was a challenge. Still, I was ready
to do whatever it took to get out of my impoverished state.

I continued to send out resumes and look for work, but alas,
nothing panned out. Then, out of the blue, a friend called. He was
moving to Albuquerque, he said. He knew I needed to earn a living,
and he wondered if I'd want to take over his landscaping business.
Would I ever! I was excited to say the least.

We met to arrange the terms of the purchase of his business. He
had half a dozen lucrative clients and a couple of trailers for hauling
around the various tools and equipment he used. We agreed to terms,
and I was off and running as a landscaper.

I needed to buy a truck to pull the trailers and to drive to my new
clients' homes, so I told my friend that if he came across the right kind

of truck, I'd be interested in buying it.

Just two hours later he called to say he'd found the right truck for me; it was old, but it was priced right and the owner had just put it up for sale. He gave me the seller's address, and I jumped right into my car and drove straight there. The truck needed some work, so the owner agreed to drop the price by half. We arranged to meet that evening and conclude the sale. During our conversation the owner said several people had vouched for me, so I didn't need to bring him a cashier's check; a personal check was fine. That felt like very positive energy, and it told me I was moving in the right direction.

But for the rest of the day one thought kept nagging me. In the past, I'd purchased a few older vehicles. Because of their ages and conditions, it seemed they were always breaking down. Man, I didn't want to get into expensive truck repairs. I simply couldn't afford them. So I asked God for a sign that I was doing the right thing, and if I got the sign I'd move forward, buy the truck, and start my new career as a landscaper.

That evening I met with the owner as planned. We got together at a restaurant and bar with a patio and a fire pit. We sat by the fire and talked a bit, and then I took a deep breath and nervously handed him my personal check. As soon as it left my hand I heard a voice in my mind say, "Go inside."

I excused myself, got up from my chair, opened the door into the restaurant – and there was my song filling my ears from the speakers mounted on the walls: "Blackbird" by the Beatles! The blackbird is associated with my namesake Saint Kevin; in fact, one of the best-known poems by the Irish Nobel laureate Seamus Heaney is called "Saint Kevin and the Blackbird." It tells of how Saint Kevin stood patiently for days while a blackbird built a nest in his hand, laid eggs, and hatched the eggs into chicks. I was positive this was the sign I'd prayed for, and it confirmed that I was on the right track. In the midst of my gratitude and relief, I grinned from ear to ear.

A few days later another miracle happened. I got a phone call from a long-time friend who volunteered at her church. The church needed a new landscape design and installation, she said. She was a board member and was available, right then, to meet with me, so I blurted out, "Ten minutes! I'll be there in ten minutes."

We met and I shared my vision for the church's facade and my thoughts about the landscaping. She said that I was just the guy the board members had been praying for. She would present my proposal to them right away. I prepared a presentation for the board, and I was selected for the job.

What a relief this was for me! Prior to this, after returning from France and after laying out hundreds of dollars for the ancient truck I'd just bought, I'd been practically destitute. Now I was engaged in a substantial undertaking – for $20,000! The arrangement with the church was that they'd pay half of the money up front, so I was able to purchase a newer and more reliable vehicle.

One year later I had a steady landscaping business with more than twenty-six clients for regular maintenance. I also developed business relationships to do landscaping for two property management companies. I was finally recovering, both spiritually and financially. I was coming back into the world.

After several months of landscaping, I finally remembered that I'd had great feelings of joy and satisfaction about landscaping work even before I'd returned from France. At that time, my joy and satisfaction must have been overheard, and Spirit predestined me to have landscaping as my employment.

It had happened when I was visiting my friends Heinrich and Ella. They lived in a rural area in a restored mill house in the tiny village of La Celle-Dunoise in Limousin in central France. During the few days I spent there, I'd helped Heinrich restack cords of wood, clean out his garden, chop down high weeds, and prune the trees that lined the front of the mill house. Heinrich had been so impressed with my energy and skills and diligence that he'd suggested I work for him, but because I wanted to return to the U.S. I'd declined.

But as I was pruning the last tree at the end of an afternoon of working on the property, I felt it. Even now, I remember the exact moment. A small stream was gurgling just a few feet away, while above my head while the sun shown through the branches of the tree as I made my final pruning cut. Finishing the job, intense feelings of accomplishment and peace and joy overcame me. A cool breeze ran across my face, and I actually spoke the words out loud with a great devotion in my heart: "God, I love landscaping."

I guess I was heard.

CHAPTER 37

ANAIS

It's not how old you are, it's how you are old.
~ *Jules Renard*

It was a hot summer in Sedona. I was landscaping out in the sun when it was 101 degrees. To make things worse, I was now fifty-five. I'd spent my recent birthday asking myself why I was doing manual labor (yard maintenance and weed pulling) in my mid-fifties. So as I suffered every day in the dirt and the intense heat, I was miserable not only about the temperature, but also about my job and my age.

In the midst of all this, for some strange reason a movie I'd once seen kept popping into my head. Called *Harold and Maude*, it's about Maude, an elderly lady who survived the Holocaust, and her friend Harold, a young man in his twenties. Although Harold is from a wealthy family, he has complex emotional problems – until he meets Maude. Maude teaches Harold about living life to its fullest and that life is the most precious gift of all. The movie is a love story about the two of them.

When I'd seen *Harold and Maude* in the 1970s, I'd been intrigued by the strange idea that a young man and an elderly woman could care so deeply for each other. I remembered clearly how each of them opened up to the other, but their love was still beyond my understanding. And the thing that puzzled me now was why this movie was so frequently on my mind.

A few days later the heat wave kept blazing and I kept feeling grumpy about my lot in life. Then I got a call from a woman who needed some landscaping clean-up in her backyard. I drove to her house and saw it was a simple job that I could assign to one of my assistants.

The woman's name was Anais, and she made sure I understood that it was pronounced "Anna-EES" with the accent on the third syllable. She was petite, perky, and vibrant, with a spark of enthusiasm in her voice. She was delighted to share that her body of eighty-seven years was in top shape. To show me how a lifetime of dancing had helped her stay toned, she insisted that I feel her flexed bicep and her upper thigh.

Anais spoke with zest about living life to the fullest and told me about her experiences. Her divorce was a cliché: at forty-nine her husband ran off with his young secretary leaving her to care for their two children, but she confessed that she'd had many lovers after that. She related how she'd gone back to college and finished her psychology degree, and she said that although it was challenging, she'd loved every minute of her classes. Hearing this was meaningful to me because I, too, had gone back to school in my fifties and finished my own psychology degree just months earlier. Also like her, I'd loved the classes, but now I faced the challenge of getting started doing work in spiritual psychology.

Anais spoke of how she'd served as a psychologist for diverse clients ranging from major Hollywood stars to young children. She showed me a binder with news clippings about being interviewed on radio stations and about a dance troupe that she'd dearly loved. Now she said she waited with happy expectation for her time to depart from this world.

She had a special gleam in her eye when she said she graduated from college at the age of fifty-five. "That was when my life began, at age fifty five," she stated. I was incredibly relieved to hear these words, because I was feeling at the end of my rope. Her life's experiences, which really began when she was the age I was now, were nothing short of miraculous. I found great comfort in them, and I felt my gloom dissipating. I could now see that being fifty-five wasn't so bad, and that it could be the beginning of great things for me.

Anais whispered her next story into my ear as though it were a secret that she didn't want anyone else to overhear. She said that next door to her lived a young lady who was single and was a part-time massage therapist. I didn't see any reason for the secret whispering until Anais got to the part where she told me that if I made an appointment for a massage, I might get a "happy ending." Hearing this I burst into laughter, and it was probably the first time in weeks that I'd had a good laugh.

Anais also told me that she was a Holocaust survivor but that she didn't like to talk about it. That was when I realized how much she was like Maude, the elderly woman in *Harold and Maude*. And I knew I'd been thinking about the movie so much lately because this elderly woman named Anais was about to come into my life.

The afternoon of storytelling and sharing flew by, and eventually it was time for me to leave for my next appointment with another client. Anais and I hugged and smiled at each other as though our souls had each just received exactly what was needed to carry us forward on our life's path. The experience of being with Anais that afternoon had elevated my spirits and given me a new outlook on life. I left there with love in my heart and a smile on my face. Before this, I had never understood how the young man in the movie was so intrigued by and in love with the elderly woman. But after that day with Anais, I did understand, and I was blessed beyond words.

CHAPTER 38

TIMOTHY GREEN

Movies and magic have always been closely associated. The very earliest people who made film were magicians.
  ~ Francis Ford Coppola

The summer heat continued unabated. In spite of my wonderful experience with Anais, it was just plain exhausting to be laboring outside in 101 degree temperatures. I was still tempted to quit the landscaping business and find a new line of work. And then I saw a film called *The Odd Life of Timothy Green*, based on a story by Frank Zappa's son, Ahmet. This film revealed to me the message that I should not give up.

The movie is about a childless couple who awaken in the middle of the night during a storm to find in their kitchen a boy named Timothy who calls them "Mom" and "Dad." Timothy is a normal child – except that he has leaves growing from his ankles. As the film progresses, through Timothy the couple learn many wonderful things about parenting and about themselves. But Timothy eventually reveals to his new parents that his lifespan will be short, and soon he is gone from their lives.

Timothy's death in the film was bittersweet for me. It was sad that he died, yet he had embodied intense unconditional love and imparted many lessons and gifts to those around him. His death reminded me when my own brother died, letting go in love.

The leaves attached to Timothy's lower legs and ankles symbolized his gifts of self to the world, to his parents, and to the young girl who helped him create beautiful "nature panels" that hung from the trees in the forest. As he expressed his own uniqueness, others were given a better understanding of nature and of unconditional divine love.

The movie spoke to me about not giving up on life, and one night as I lay in bed I recalled a book by Wayne Muller. It was entitled *Legacy of the Heart,* and I had it right there under a pile of other books on my nightstand. I dug it out and the first thing I noticed was a leaf on its cover – like the ones on Timothy's ankles in the movie. As I lifted up the book to read, it fell open to page 71. There I read the following two sentences that I had highlighted years before:

Our purpose is not to eliminate these voices but to understand them with open, mindful attention. And then . . . You may say, "I will not judge or hurt myself with thoughts or criticisms. I will now treat myself only with Loving Kindness."

I knew in that moment of reading that I was to let go of the negative voices in my head. I also understood that I was no longer to allow destructive thoughts to break down my enthusiasm for life – and for landscaping. With a sense of peace I lay my head back onto my pillow and fell soundly asleep.

The following morning at a client's house, I found that my client, too, had seen the movie about Timothy Green. We spoke briefly about our reactions to it, and about our own life experiences regarding loved ones who had passed on.

At lunchtime, I was again reminded of the film. At a restaurant I sat down in its courtyard and listened to the relaxing sound of a fountain flowing quietly into a small pond. As I looked up, I saw that the clouds were grey and ominous, so I scooted my chair and table under a large tree nearby. And there in the tree was the same leaf and heart design that Timothy had worn in the film. I smiled and felt happy, in spite of the coming rain. I could weather the storm.

Speaking of storms, a few nights later I saw another film, *The Perfect Storm.* One scene in particular captured my attention. It showed a female violinist handing everyone heart-shaped leaves; then on her violin she played rich low tones representing moss, and lovely high notes representing tall grasses, performing all this with her violin and interpreting the magnificent sounds of nature.

These experiences represent to me how we need to be open to the messages that come to us. Time and time again, whether through books, film, music, people, or direct experiences with nature, I'm reminded of the beauty all around us. I'm also reminded of the love within each of us and the goodness that we are to share with one another while we're here. That is our gift to each other and to the world.

CHAPTER 39

IT COMES IN THREES:
COLLETTE, SERENA AND ARCHANGEL MICHAEL

The Archangel Michael took supreme command. He reassured their minds
by his serenity
  ~ Anatole France

In the midst doing landscaping on a daily basis, I still thought that
someday I might write a book.
But life had taken over. I had to build a business to have a steady
income. And this required long hours of landscape installations and
maintenance, not to mention ancillary duties, such as billing, buying
supplies, and keeping my tools in good working order.

Sometimes I wondered if I'd ever get to leave the landscaping
business and do the work I desired, the work I'd trained for, and the
work I felt I was meant to do. There was also the issue of where Spirit
wanted me to live. I'd often remember a trip to California with my
girlfriend Sarah when we'd spent my birthday in Santa Barbara right
at the beach. I'd felt this would be the perfect place for me to establish
a retreat center for couples counseling once I'd completed my master's
degree in spiritual psychology. But now I'd had the degree for a year,
and I was still in Arizona.

So I sought advice from a woman named Tanya. She was an
insightful psychic who'd done readings for me in the past. I visited her
once or twice a year, and I typically asked for guidance about my job

and my relationship – as well as when I would start doing the spiritual psychology work I'd trained for.

On this day she wasn't available, and the concierge suggested that I instead see a new psychic reader named Collette. I was a little unsettled by this suggestion, so I just looked at the woman behind the counter and said, "Thanks, but I don't want to see anyone except Tanya." Nevertheless, the woman was insistent, telling me Collette had had astounding psychic gifts since childhood and was very accurate in her readings. So I finally capitulated, saying, "I'm willing to have a session with her – but a short one."

A few minutes later a young attractive woman with multiple tattoos entered, introduced herself, and sat down. As she settled into her chair, Collette shared her intention to do a reading for me. I acknowledged that I was ready.

Almost immediately she began to whip her head from side to side in a very strange manner. She opened her eyes wide, looked at me, and said, "This is unusual. Archangels almost never show up in my readings, and they never appear this early." Then she stared into my eyes and said in a very stern voice, "Archangel Michael is demanding to know why you haven't written your book. People are waiting for it."

My jaw dropped! I felt like a little boy being scolded. Those words were direct and powerful, and I knew, in that moment, that I couldn't avoid the book any longer.

The next statement out of Collette's mouth was: "Do you know you're going to live between Santa Barbara and Big Sur? You'll start up a retreat center with another man. You won't have to do all the work by yourself any longer. You and he will combine efforts." She added, "You're going to California during the first few weeks in October."

My mind was spinning. This woman who'd never met me and who'd been living in Sedona for only a few weeks seemed to know all about me. I was getting the confirmation that I needed. I knew Collette's statements were true and that I needed to get started on my book right away.

As we continued our session, I felt very strongly was that Collette wouldn't be in Sedona much longer and would be leaving soon. But I didn't get a chance to tell her this, and it didn't seem to matter in that moment. (Some days later I called the shop only to learn she'd indeed moved from Sedona.)

After my reading with Collette, I went for dinner to a local Italian bistro. I took a seat at my usual table, and I began telling Serena, my friend and waitress, about my reading with Collette. Serena was wide-eyed as she listened with full attention.

After I finished, Serena looked at me and said, "How many times do you need to be hit on the head with this?"

I stared back at her. "Okay," I said. "I will start writing right after dinner." She took my order and walked away, and as I waited for my meal, I used my smart phone to check Facebook. I went first to the alumni page of the school where I'd gotten my master's degree. And as the page opened, there it was:

Filling my screen was a beautiful pale-blue light and a message from Archangel Michael. It read, "Do you know what Archangel Michael is telling you? You need to step up and do what it is that you have been called to do!"

This was my third reminder. Within a single day, I'd had one from Collette, one from Serena, and now one from Archangel Michael himself.

So I went home right after dinner and began writing this book.

CHAPTER 40

Reverend Theresa

*If we accept that sound is vibration and we know that vibration touches
every part of our physical being, then we understand that sound is heard
not only through our ears but through every cell in our bodies.*
  ~ Dr. Mitchell Gaynory

I first heard of Reverend Theresa from a friend who recommended that I do a session with her. Reverend Theresa did healing
work with sound. The idea intrigued me, so I contacted her for
more information. After a brief conversation with her, I scheduled
an appointment.

As the day of the appointment approached she contacted me to
indicate that her husband would be co-facilitating the session with
her. I was surprised and wondered what it would be like to have a
session with both of them together. Until that time, I'd had healing
work done on me by only one person at a time. But I relaxed into the
idea and reassured myself about whatever it was that would happen.
I also reminded myself that miracles often happen outside of our
comfort zone.

The two arrived at my home. Reverend Theresa let me know
how the session would work and that she'd use various songs along
with melodious sounds, musical instruments, chanting, drumming,
and other modalities that she and her husband had perfected over
many years.

I stretched out on a massage table in my living room, and as the session began, I felt old experiences and old energies being peeled away in layers from my body. I could feel my physical and emotional bodies tuning into and releasing old hurts and blockages that had plagued me in the past. Midway through I felt my arms rise up toward the ceiling with no effort on my part. It was as if someone else had grasped my wrists and forearms and was lifting them upward.

The experience approached its high point, and I was at the peak of releasing negativity. Then, as the music, the chanting, and the body-work drew to a close, I felt as if my body were surrounded by a golden bubble of light. For several years I'd intentionally visualized a golden bubble during meditations, but I had never seen the golden sphere so vividly in my mind's eye. Next I entered a realm outside of the golden sphere, a world of angels, archangels, and guides. This was like nothing I'd ever read about or experienced. The beings were delighted to be watching all of humankind going through our diverse experiences, and they were waiting patiently, with great joy, to enter our world when it was appropriate. And as I experienced this, I could feel myself sharing in their bliss.

Moments later, a huge blackness or void appeared to the upper right of the angelic sphere. I entered this dark void, and as I did, I was consumed by intense feelings of wholeness and expansiveness. I was filled with an intense profound love, and I knew with total confidence that this was the basis of existence.

I was aware that I had traveled into Love itself. I felt the love of a parent looking down on all of creation. I felt the love of a parent for a child or children. I felt the love and compassion and protectiveness that the parent would have as the child stumbled or stubbed a toe or even experienced something far more painful. And all were loved equally. Simultaneously, a love for and within myself surrounded and filled me, and consumed me with its positive energy.

I slowly came back to conscious awareness there on the massage table in the presence of Reverence Theresa and her husband. I knew that their sounds, music, chanting, and other modalities had helped me to achieve this new realization, and I knew that it is with the assistance of others that we most easily find our way back home.

CHAPTER 41

DIVINE ASSISTANCE

Coincidence is God's way of remaining anonymous.
  ~ Albert Einstein

I'd been divinely inspired to start writing my book. I wanted to make a difference and to reach a large number of people. But I'd never written a book before. Previously I'd made every excuse to procrastinate. But now I was truly ready to get going.

I knew I could do the writing part. But I knew nothing about putting together a book beyond writing a draft. To finish the book and get it published, I needed three kinds of assistance: an inspirational role model, an editor, and an illustrator.

So I asked Spirit to send me these individuals whose help I needed.

One afternoon following a hard day of landscaping I decided that after going home to take a shower, I'd take myself out to a nice dinner. I wanted to treat myself for working so hard, and I drove up and down Highway 89A, the main road in West Sedona, trying to lock in on a good restaurant. But I couldn't come up with any type of food I felt like eating. Nothing appealed to me.

As I continued driving up and down 89A, I heard a little familiar voice say, "Go to Enchantment Resort." I knew the resort offered fine dining, so I turned the car around and headed straight there. I pulled into the parking lot and looked around at the majestic red rocks surrounding me, took a deep breath, and walked up the stairs to the restaurant.

The hostess took me out onto the patio. As I made my way to the table, I noticed a young man sitting by himself. He looked a bit dark – dark in the Gothic sense, with black hair, fingernails painted black, and a lot of tattoos. Yet inside my head, Spirit told me to sit down next to him and "Hold the Light."

Only moments later, he turned around in his chair and we started to talk. He shared with me that he was there on a sort of personal retreat. He spoke about how he'd just come from a long telephone conversation with his manager. I wondered what it was he did for a living, but I didn't pursue this, and our conversation turned to diverse topics ranging from his childhood to his relationship with his wife and children. I listened intently.

He eventually revealed to me that he was a novelist from Austin, that he'd written forty best-selling books, and that a couple of them had been made into Hollywood movies. Wow, was I excited and filled with gratitude! This was the role model I needed to inspire me to write my book. And he said that when I'd walked onto the patio, he knew that he was supposed to talk with me.

We spoke together for an hour. I wanted to respect his privacy and his time, so I eventually wrapped up the conversation and handed him my card. I told him to call me if he wanted to continue our talk some other time.

Leaving the restaurant I realized that Spirit had sent him to help me write my book, but I hadn't asked him for any information about writing or publishing. Nevertheless, I was happy that I'd had the opportunity to meet him and have the conversation we'd had. I knew it was a blessing, and I thanked Spirit for making it happen.

I was surprised a day or so later when he called. We talked a bit, and then we made plans to meet for dinner at a restaurant called Elote, an authentic Mexican restaurant and one of my favorites. A day later we spent another evening on the patio at Heartline Cafe.

These evenings went really well as we laughed and swapped stories about our lives. I shared with him a lot of the experiences I've written about in this book. I knew I'd met a kindred soul, and I was confident that he felt the same way. He told me a lot about his life and the struggles he'd faced getting to where he was. I felt enormous respect for the fact that he'd worked very hard for many years and devoted his life to the craft of writing. Perhaps the most surprising thing he said was that he had million-dollar book deals, drove a custom Aston Martin, and lived in a 10,000 square foot home – yet he was terrified of losing it all.

The most profound words he said during our final conversation were these: "When you write your book, write as if no one is going to read it but you."

For days after our last meeting, though, I continued to focus on how fearful he was about losing everything he'd gained. On the following Sunday I went for a massage to help ground me from the exhilarating experience of meeting my new role model. An hour into the massage a surge of emotion swept through me from the depths of my soul. I took a gasp for air and then tears rolled down my cheeks. And a message came thundering through in my mind: "You are not your success!" I took another deep breath and realized I was being reminded not to become attached to anything, not even success.

So I began to write my book, but as I did, I realized I needed someone who could help me with nuts-and-bolts things like: How many pages should it be? How should the book be structured? In what way should it be distributed or printed? Should I present it in ebook form, or in print? And if in print, should it be a hardcover or a softcover book? As these questions swirled in my mind, once again I asked Spirit for help. I also asked that Spirit send someone who lived locally and had time to work with me.

The following Sunday I took a workshop on emotional release work. I didn't enjoy it, and throughout the workshop I kept hearing that little voice say, "Get out of here and go to lunch." In response, at the break I headed to my usual lunch spot, the Secret Garden Cafe. I arrived after the lunch hour was over, and the only other person on the patio was a woman seated by herself at an adjacent table. After a while, she turned to me and said she admired my bracelet and wanted to know its significance. I explained that the lettering read "Om Nami Shiva" in Sanskrit, and that it signified auspicious beginnings. We then talked about our love for horses and about the fact that I was writing a book, and then we introduced ourselves.

Her name was Cassandra, she was the author of several books, and she was a writing professor at Northern Arizona University. She said she'd be happy to assist me by answering my nuts-and-bolts questions and by editing my book. Once again, divine assistance had brought the right person into my life.

Now I had my inspirational role model. And I had my editor. But I still needed an illustrator to do the layout of the book's contents, the front cover, and the internal artwork. I held in my mind that I needed an artist. And I asked Spirit to assist me. I didn't demand help in any way; I simply asked for what I needed.

The right person crossed my path when I least expected it.

I was at the post office. Christmas was coming soon, and the parking lot was crowded, so the cars were all parked right next to one another. As I got out of my SUV the woman in the next car rolled her window down and said, "Your lights are on." I replied "They turn off by themselves," and I thanked her. I walked into the post office thinking how nice it was for her to tell me about my lights, and in the back of my head a bell rang. I thought, "She looks so familiar."

I was heading back to my car when I saw her again. I told her she looked familiar but I couldn't place her. She answered that her name was Peggy and that she was the painter who rented the artist's studio next to my former girlfriend's studio space where they both used to paint. I smiled and nodded as I realized who she was. We talked briefly about how things were going and how Sarah was doing.

We walked toward my car and continued talking, and she asked me what I was up to. I replied, "I'm writing a book" and went on to explain what the book was about. I mentioned that I'd been inspired by a successful author I'd met a short time earlier at Enchantment Resort, and that a writing professor from Northern Arizona University was going to help with the editing. Almost immediately Peggy reached into her purse, pulled out her business card, and handed it to me.

"I'm an illustrator," she said. She mentioned that her company, "Indigo Designo," had done some book covers and illustrations for Osho, the Indian mystic and guru also known as Bhagwan Shree Rajneesh. She offered her services to design and layout my book and to do the front cover. We said goodbye to one another with

235

the intention of collaborating on the book in the near future.

   As I drove away, I thanked Spirit for providing divine assistance. The three people I needed had been brought to me: the role model, the editor, and the artist. I was ecstatically happy, and I relaxed with the knowledge that I was provided for, and that my needs were taken care of.

CHAPTER 42

CHANNELING SPIRIT, PART ONE

Automatic Writing: Writing . . . produced from a subconscious,
and/or external and/or spiritual source without conscious awareness
of the content.
    ~ Wikipedia

And so I started to write this book. One day in late August as I was writing, something unusual happened. It began when I ran out of ink and had to search for another pen. Later I recalled only this annoying incident. I didn't even remember what I had written that day.

When I was done scribbling, I took my notebook upstairs and put it on my nightstand. The next day I began writing in a new notebook, so this one sat there at my bedside for the next few weeks.

That night I had a lucid and unsettling dream. It was so real! I'd had scary dreams where the fright would awaken me. But this was different.

Over the years I've met many people who've had unexplainable experiences with beings from other worlds. When listening to them tell their stories, I know I've given each of them a deer-in-the-headlights look, because I'd never had such experiences and I didn't know what to think. But now, amazingly, I'm the one telling the story. You might be giving me a deer-in-the-headlights look, but nevertheless, I want to tell you what happened.

I dreamed I was in a large domed building. My surroundings were bathed in soft white light with a touch of aqua-blue. Somehow I knew the enormous dome was an intergalactic way station or terminal. During the dream I saw many entities from other solar systems. The one I remember best was a tall man with blond hair that hung past his shoulders. He was dressed in an aqua-blue uniform with gold shoulder epaulets.

I stood there before him, and I knew he was trying to share a message with me. The message was that all people on earth were going to die. To him, this was the natural order of things. And I sensed that this wouldn't be a physical death. It would, instead, be a shift to a new level of consciousness, one that mankind had not yet known.

When I awoke from the dream, I immediately thought of the Hopi belief that a blond man with long hair had visited the earth from a distant galaxy. For me, the dream was tied to this and to many prophesies I'd read. For example, the Hopi believe that soon a great destruction is coming – a time of fires, diseases, and death. After this happens, the Hopi's "Lost White Brother," a man named Pahana, will return and will help the Hopi rebuild. The Hopi say his return marks a new stage in human existence: "the Dawn of the Fifth World." I also thought of Nostradmus's prophecies about the end of the world, and of the Mayan calendar that had ended just a few months before, on December 21, 2012.

Meanwhile this dream perplexed me on many levels. As mentioned before, I'd known several people who'd supposedly seen UFOs, who'd supposedly encountered aliens, who'd supposedly even been abducted – but I had not. Yet my attitude was neutral on the subject, and I'd always wondered, "Why can't they exist?" Just because I hadn't seen or experienced these things didn't mean they weren't real.

So I kept an open mind about my dream. Three weeks later I heard my intuition, which is that small voice inside me, say, "Pick up the notebook by the bed and read it."

The notebook fell open to the pages from that day when my pen ran out of ink. I read what I had written, and it was strange, because the words seemed to be have written by someone else. I'd spent the previous two years taking classes and writing papers that were intended to open me to a different level of experiencing the world. And now I had before me pages filled with a wisdom that blew me away. And it was in my own handwriting.

I'd created what is called "automatic writing." This is writing produced when Spirit takes control of the writer and reveals messages. It's a type of channeling; the writer becomes a channel or conduit for a being or spirit who communicates information via writing.

The information I'd written helped me to understand the universe, human experience, and human existence on a very different level of consciousness that what I'd previously known.

Here's a quote from my channeling:

> *Call Galapagos island of Giles*
> *Call Galeopsian Sea*
> *Call Trisoflopian . . .*
> *See foam green of color, transmit it, be it,*
> *feel it and let the energy take you.*
> *Don't be afraid.*

A few days passed, and I decided to look up the Galapagos island of Giles on the Internet. I'd heard of the Galapagos Islands, of course, but I wasn't sure if the island of Giles even existed. So I was amazed when I saw a Website about the Galapagos island of Giles!

I went to the site and found breathtaking photos of indigo water, a stunning coastline, and intriguing sea creatures such as turtles. They were all gorgeous. My eyes scanned the thumbnail images and suddenly, there it was: a picture of the tall blond man in his aqua-blue uniform and the space craft that I had seen in my dream. I was astounded. My mind reeled with excitement and curiosity as I wondered what this all meant and how it was connected to me.

Two days later, after I'd meditated on all this, asking that the significance be explained to me, another remarkable event occurred.

It took place on a weekend afternoon as I was walking around the shopping area where I'd had my tobacco store. This was rare for me because, having lost my retail business, this was the last place I wanted to go; it brought back painful memories of what I'd lost. Indeed, whenever I even thought of going back to my shop's location I felt uneasy and unsettled. But nevertheless, something was calling me to do this.

On this day a New Age festival called the Gump Fest was taking place. It wasn't something I'd normally have attended. But for some reason I had the desire to go and explore the booths positioned in front of my former business.

Just a few feet from the doorway of my tobacco store was a booth with a white tent over its table. Inside was a computer screen. And on the screen was a picture of the tall blond man and the space ship I'd seen in my dream and on the Website!

I needed to know what this was all about. So I talked with several of the people at the booth. They seemed to know all about this tall blond man and his mission. They called him a "Galactic Avatar." They said he and his people were from a distance "Star System." They said his people would assist our people and our planet during the "Shift" that has already begun. They added that the message of these people was one of peace and that we are all one, no matter what universe we're from.

Several others who were staffing the booth said they'd gotten the call to live in Sedona. Some of them told me stories of how they'd left successful careers behind. They'd come here to spread the word and they were, they said, helping to hold the "Light," a frequency of energy, and to assist earth and its people during the "Shift."

What they were saying didn't seem too far-fetched to me. My own path to Sedona some seventeen years earlier was similar to what they described. So I bought their T-shirt and their CD, and although I still wasn't sure how these experiences all fit together, I headed for home again feeling grateful for having encountered these people and still trying to integrate all that had recently happened.

CHAPTER 43

Channeling Spirit, Part Two

Yesterday is but today's memory, and tomorrow is today's dream.
~ *Khalil Gibran*

The following week I visited my teacher, Grandfather Morning Owl.

I explained to him what had happened during my dream, my journal writing, and the event that took place in front of my former store. As he listened intently, Grandfather showed no surprise. Instead, the smile on his face told me that he perfectly understood what I was saying.

He walked over to the bookshelf that held his many books and memorabilia. He lifted something from the shelf and held it clenched in his fist. He said, "Close your eyes and open your hand." I did as he said and felt a small object that was cool to my touch. "Just feel the stone," he said. So I did for the next few minutes. Then he took back the stone and told me to open my eyes. As I did, he began to relate his own experiences from thirty-five years earlier that had occurred on the same intergalactic station in my dream.

He shared with me that he'd allowed only a few people to hold the stone, and that nearly all of them had told him about their journey to the same intergalactic space station. Most of these people, he said, had described the place from the outside, and only a few, including myself, had actually been inside the dome. He noted that many years ago he'd placed the stone into the hands of a NASA scientist without telling him what it signified, and the scientist had mentally (and perhaps even physically, in a sense) traveled across the galaxies to the place I'd described.

Grandfather said he'd come across this stone while on a walkabout with aboriginal elders in Australia. He'd been guided to a spot among the rocks of the desert, and when he'd consulted the elders about this place, they'd said it was a gateway or portal where one could enter another dimension and astral travel. One of the elders asked how he'd found the portal, and Grandfather said his heart had led him to it. Another elder noted that given the right time and the right energy, a person could go to the place and disappear.

Hearing this story led me to share with Grandfather another dream I'd had.

In my dream I was trying to open a large rounded Romanesque-style doorway that was about six feet wide and eight feet high. I knew that this doorway led to a special place, and I wanted to enter. Above and around the doorway were strange symbols: circles, squares, and many other shapes. I knew that if I pulled the symbols out or turned them in the correct sequence, the door would open for me. But I couldn't figure out which ones to pull or move. I was stumped. In the dream, Grandfather was there with me standing on my right side. He reached up and turned one of the symbols, and he pulled out another. The door opened.

After I explained my dream, Grandfather said I was being shown the importance my work would have in the future. He said I had only to be patient and wait for everything to align itself – just as it had for him, thirty-five years ago.

CHAPTER 44

"SEE" FOAM GREEN

We must become so alone that we withdraw into our innermost self. . . .
Then our solitude is overcome and we are no longer alone, for we find that
our innermost self is the spirit that is God, the indivisible. . . .
And we know ourselves to be one with all beings.
   ~ Hermann Hesse

I continued to be perplexed by the meaning of the "channeled" material in my notebook from that "automatic writing" session when my pen had run out of ink. Part of what I had written read as follows: *"Call Trisoflopian. . . . See foam green of color, transmit it, be it, feel it, and let the energy take you. Don't be afraid."* This was the last entry of the channeling and writing session that my hand placed on paper. And it wasn't a mistake that I had spelled "sea" in "see foam green" as "see." Instead, it was a reference to a new level of awareness.

For the next few days I meditated on the color seafoam green. I'd written those pages around my birthday, and at about that same time I'd gone to one of the local crystal stores searching for a seafoam-green-colored stone. At the time I hadn't quite understood why I was so intrigued with this color. But it was beginning to make sense to me now. The "see" in "seefoam" meant that I needed to open my eyes and "see" – and open my heart, as well.

Nevertheless, I still didn't understand the complete meaning of the words "see foam green." I was confident that something would be revealed to me; I just didn't know how or when. So I released my questions into the universe, knowing that the answer would be divulged to me in the perfect way and at the perfect time.

I continued to meditate daily on the color of the ocean, seafoam green, and on the alternate spelling I'd used in my notebook. I even revisited the crystal store and stood staring at stones in the seafoam color. During my work week, I did my best to hold that thought and that color in my mind, but more often than not, it seemed to slip away, replaced by another vision that frequently popped into my head.

In this other vision I saw myself opening my heart at Sedona's Unity Spiritual Center. Two women came to my side and held me in a place of love. And I allowed myself to express my emotions regardless of what others thought.

The following Sunday morning I was at the Spiritual Center listening to the leader, Uriel, then strange things began to happen to me. I became absorbed – utterly absorbed – by the lecture, the music, the sounds, and the energy in the room. Uriel had selected a song called "Hummingbird." It was by Seals and Croft, and it had helped me through some of my most challenging times as a teenager.

Meanwhile, Uriel spoke about "fragmenting," a term I'd heard in my dream, from one of the beings in the intergalactic space station. "Fragmenting" means getting bits and pieces of information that seem disjointed yet urgently compelling; they eventually come together in a moment of grace to form a complete and meaning-ful truth. When Uriel spoke of fragmenting, his words hit home for me, because at times the seemingly unrelated bits and pieces of data coming into my consciousness were so great that I thought I would lose my mind. Imagine finding a few pieces of a puzzle daily, knowing that the completed image would change your life or rock your world or even save another's life, but you have no ability to gather the remaining pieces!

Uriel explained how this fragmenting could cause mental unrest, deep confusion, and even possibly psychosis. As he spoke I noticed that Sarah, the woman with whom I'd just ended a long-term soulful relationship, and Benedict, a friend of ours, had entered and had taken seats not too far away from me. I was glad to see them.

But as the talk continued, my body began to tremble. I couldn't catch my breath. I gasped for air, and I knew that something, some emotion, was rising up from my psyche. I also knew that what was happening was related to my vision of opening my heart at the Spiritual Center. I decided not to hold back; something big was pushing through, and I would permit it. As I did, my tears began to flow and I allowed the experience to happen, but as quietly as possible in the small sanctuary. Two ladies touched me briefly to let me know they were there. I was grateful for their support.

Uriel's talk continued, as did my emotional release. I committed to the healing that was taking place inside me, and I opened to it. By now my body was shaking uncontrollably. Then out of the corner of my eye I noticed that Sarah and Benedict were leaving. I held them in love and put my head back down.

Moments later, when most of the people had left the service, I felt a hand on my back. I saw Sarah kneeling at my side, and I knew it was Benedict at my back. I sobbed even harder. They caressed my legs and back for some time without saying a word. A short while after that they helped me stand up. My legs trembled, and they supported me as I walked out into the sunlight.

I rounded the side of the building and sat on the ground. I slid my hands into the gravel to ground myself in Mother Earth's energy. As I leaned over, just inches away from the ground, my nose was running from all the crying. I felt Sarah's fingers reach across my wet nose to remove all that was streaming down, and I heard her say softly, "Now, if that isn't love." In that moment I felt the full connection and unconditional love we'd had for each other through many lifetimes.

Finally I regained my composure and felt sufficiently present in my body to drive. I gave Sarah and Benedict each a kiss on the lips and an embrace filled with love and appreciation. Then I headed home.

On entering my condo, as I tried to climb the flight of stairs to my bedroom on the second floor, I knew that I wouldn't make it. The landing midway up the stairs became my resting spot. I lay down under the skylight and the large wooden Buddha on the wall. As I lay there on my back, I looked up and saw millions of particles of light, like snowflakes, falling from the skylight onto me. I opened my arms, accepted them, and fell into a deep sleep.

250

A short time later I awoke with a knowledge of what had just happened to me and through me. I had an awareness deep within me. I could "see," as in "see foam green." And in a second's flash I realized that Uriel, Unity's spiritual leader, had been wearing a seafoam green shirt at the service. I also recognized that, as in my vision, two women had appeared by my side and held me in unconditional love.

I knew that my heart was now open to this unconditional love: to receiving it, and to giving it. In the past I'd had experiences that had brought me to the edge of opening my heart, but I'd held back – I hadn't been ready. This morning, however, at the Spiritual Center, I hadn't held back from this healing. Instead, I'd allowed it to happen. My vision had become my reality . . . and this was just the beginning!

CHAPTER 45

SOUL GROUPS

*I seem to have loved you in numberless forms, numberless times, in life after
life, in age after age forever. He who wants to do good, knocks at the gate.
He who loves, finds the door open.*
     ~ *Rabindranath Tagore*

Most people are familiar with the concept of "soulmates." These
are individuals on similar spiritual paths, who may have been
together for many lifetimes. Plato discusses this idea in *The Symposium*;
it's also present in the Jewish Talmud, and in the writings of the mystic
Edgar Cayce.

Akin to the idea of soulmates is the idea of "twin flames." Twin
flames form a balance of male and female energies, and a twin flame is
the other half of one's soul. Although the twin flame makes one whole,
it is also a complete soul in its own right. It is said that when one meets
his or her twin flame, the person knows this instantly.

A similar concept is that of soul groups: people who reincarnate
together.

A soul group is a gathering of souls. To deepen their experiences
on earth, they come together via diverse roles and various walks of
life. Some soul groups find each other lifetime after lifetime. They
encounter aspects of their being that must be relived, remembered,
or healed and the wisdom imparted realized. Time after time mothers
become sons, sons become mothers, those who were wealthy become

poor, those who were subservient become powerful, and so on.

A soul group is, then, a group of beings who help us learn life lessons. Soul groups enable us to meet the people we need to meet at important times in our lives, and not by coincidence. Soulmates or twin flames are part of the soul group, but one's soulmate/twin flame might not be present in one's current incarnation. For example, a soulmate may remain in the ethereal realm to provide otherworldly help and spiritual guidance. Alternatively, an individual may have been called to be present in this incarnation and may have chosen to come without his or her soulmate. Not everyone from the soul group is present in a given lifecycle at the same time. Nevertheless, every member of the soul group, including the soulmate/twin flame, is always present for an individual in heart and in spirit.

The first time I encountered the concept of soul groups was when I was a guide for a Jeep tour company. I drove a Jeep taking groups of tourists to interesting spots around Sedona. During the tour I'd share information about flora and fauna, or relate the history of the area, or perform native ceremonies. One day as I was driving some English tourists I struck up a conversation with them. We talked about various spiritual phenomena, and I noted that one woman stood out from the group. When we stopped for a restroom break, she and I began to talk one on one.

I told her about a recent experience I'd had with Sarah. We'd been close friends for five years and had just begun our romantic relationship. One day, on the Summer Solstice, we'd each felt a veil being lifted from between us. That day Sarah and I discussed the ethereal realm that existed outside of everyday reality. We talked about locusts and how they represented a window to this other world. We spent all evening together, sharing what we'd experienced about each other over several lifetimes. It was like opening the Akashic or mystical records of our lives together.

For many years I'd prayed for a woman with whom I could experience the level of love and dross that Jesus and Mary Magdalene had experienced. I asked that I might have such a woman in my life for at least five years, and that she'd teach me things. Sarah had taught me a lot, including information about nutrition and how to eat in a healthier way. So it seemed I'd found the woman I'd prayed for.

Now, as I spoke to the Englishwoman, I shared my opinion that Sarah and I were twin flames. I admitted that I was so deeply in love I could barely contain love's magnitude. In response, the woman began to tell me about her understanding of soul groups.

She said those from the same soul group are here to help the others along life's path. However, she said that souls from the same soul group should not be together in the same lifetime. This confused me, and because of the love that recently had opened to Sarah and me, I couldn't accept that this might be true.

Nevertheless, I stored the information in my memory bank. I knew that something else would eventually be revealed that would clear up the confusion for me.

CHAPTER 46

Past Lives

It is love and the lover that live eternally. Don't lend the heart to anything else; all else is borrowed.

~ Rumi

Before Sarah and I began a romantic relationship, we'd had a five-year friendship. During that time, I'd had several experiences that seemed to take both of us back to other lifetimes.

For example, one day in my front yard I noticed two beautiful scarabs touching each other's bodies on a branch in a fig tree. In that moment I was mentally transported back to a time in Ancient Egypt when Sarah and I were together. I also knew that I wasn't supposed to capture them in this life time. They needed their freedom. When I told Sarah of this experience later, she became tearful and I knew she was remembering the same incarnation.

At other times, as we held each other in loving embrace, we could see each other's face in a lifetime as Native Americans or during the American Civil War. One day she even called me by a name from that era, "Morgan." On another day she said she didn't want me to leave her during this lifetime. I felt that she wasn't talking about a breakup, but about a death, and I sensed that I'd committed suicide when I'd known her in a past lifetime.

So during powerful moments, we both realized we'd had other lifetimes together. Sometimes when looking at her face I'd have a fleeting vision of being with her in another part of the world. And she said she'd glimpsed me in other lifetimes as well.

Over the past five years I'd been intrigued by these experiences and by the concept of past or parallel lifetimes. Why did I get a specific glimpse here or there? Were these memories or flashes showing up to remind me of something? Or to teach me an important lesson? I sensed that on a deep level these experiences would reveal a sense of love, gratitude, or pain, and that both Sarah and I would benefit from the revelations.

One evening as I spoke with my friend Tariana, I shared a dream I'd had a few years earlier. The dream was set somewhere in Egypt – or in some other hot, arid, desert climate, perhaps even Ancient Mesopotamia. Sarah was being stoned to death. I wanted to save her, and I was willing to give my life up for hers. As I covered her body with mine to protect her, I could feel the excruciating pain of fist-sized jagged sandstone rocks on my left side, breaking my ribs. It was so real and lucid that it startled me awake. Even now, I remember it as though I dreamed it yesterday.

After I shared my dream with Tariana, she exclaimed, "That happened because of adultery!"

Tariana had a good grasp of history, and I knew she was right. I was so stunned that I gasped and felt overcome with emotion. I knew, in that moment, that I was opening to the truth of what had happened in a lifetime long ago. Tariana began to speak again, but I was so overwhelmed that I asked her to let me catch my breath so this realization could integrate with my psyche. I didn't want to rush into the next sentence.

I sat quietly for the next couple of minutes, and I felt my sphere of consciousness open. I let this new truth anchor itself deep within me. And as I went deeper, I began to understand why I couldn't say no to Sarah in this lifetime. Finally Tariana and I began to speak again, and we explored what I was to learn from this my dream.

During our conversation I realized that I'd given my power away many lifetimes ago. But now it was time to accept that these past-life memories had surfaced to help me heal myself and reclaim my power. By doing so I was honoring both Sarah and myself.

As the conversation with Tariana continued, I was filled with a new wisdom. My heart and mind came together, and a healing release took place throughout my body and my mind. I was also filled with gratitude for reclaiming a lost part of myself.

I knew now I could now create loving boundaries in this lifetime. And I could honor myself. In so doing, I was more open to love, both for others and for myself.

I was now relieved of any lingering attachments. I was able to let go. I could allow Sarah to be on her own soul's path of learning and be grateful for it. She was my loving equal and teacher, and I was hers.

When I wrote about this experience later, another realization dawned on me. In all of our text messages and emails during the past five years, Sarah and I had each used a unique closing. These were fun for us at the time, but now they revealed a deeper meaning.

Each time we said goodbye via email or text, her closing words to me were:

"Love me. . . ."

And mine to her were:

"Love me2"

I'd never realized it until now, but we both sincerely wanted to be loved. Even our texts and emails had asked for it.

CHAPTER 47

A Warning from an Angel

Believers look up — take courage. The angels are nearer than you think.
~ *Billy Graham*

When I got involved with Sarah, she was still in another relationship. Because of this, early in our romance while waiting for a plane I had a warning from an angel.

My time with Sarah was limited because of her other relationship, and so I planned to fly to New York to meet her when she returned from her trip to Egypt. I'd decided to do this because I wanted to spend a full night with her without interruption and consummate our relationship. As I headed to the airport I recognized that our physical intimacy could cause great pain to the other person in her life. But at the same time, I longed to be with her. I was torn because I'd never been in a love triangle before. But something inside of me couldn't turn back.

As I waited for my plane, I recalled a story about an elderly Hawaiian woman, a shaman, who had nursed a young man back to health after a surfing accident. Moments later an elderly man and woman sat down next to me. Almost immediately the man left, and the woman and I began to talk. I told her why I was going to New York, and I told her I knew what I was doing could be a source of another's pain but that I couldn't turn around and go home. I said, "This is the love I've been praying and waiting for!"

The woman then told me something about herself. She revealed to me that she was headed back home to Hawaii and that her life had paralleled mine in many ways just years earlier.

She went on to say, without hesitation, that she was an angel sent by God.

She said she was sent to tell me to go home. She said my trip to see Sarah was about sex and not about love, and that I would eventually experience great pain because of this experience.

I knew she was right. I acknowledged the truth on so many levels of what she was saying. But I couldn't turn back. To do so would, I felt, be an abandonment of the profound love I'd just found.

The plane was delayed. And delayed again. And again. With each delay, the woman reminded me that I had another chance to do the right thing – to turn around and go home. But each time I simply shook my head and replied, "No. I must go."

Finally, my plane was ready for boarding. The woman smiled and bid me farewell. As the flight departed, I felt that I was being torn in two directions. But still I continued toward New York.

When we finally landed, the captain announced that an aircraft had broken down on the runway in front of us and it would be another hour before we got to the gate. By now it was nearly 8 p.m. I thought to myself, "Are you crazy? You only have a few hours to be with her. Is this worth it?" But in my mind and heart, I heard a resounding "Yes."

The challenges didn't stop there. I forgot the name of the hotel where we were to meet. In the taxi I told the driver I couldn't remember the name but that the hotel I wanted was next to the airport. I asked him not to go to Manhattan. Nevertheless, he drove onto the freeway and headed toward downtown Manhattan. I said, "Turn around. The hotel is next to the airport." But he said that because he was now on the freeway, he had to find the right exit ramp before he could turn around. After another ten minutes of driving toward the city, and I finally remembered the name of the hotel and told him to go there.

At the hotel he said I owed him forty dollars. I gave him a twenty-dollar bill, saying he'd ignored my request not to drive toward the city and I wasn't going to pay him for that part of the trip. Soon he was yelling at me in two languages and threatening to call the police. I walked away from him into the hotel, but he followed me, screaming. In retrospect, I see that this encounter was one of many signs, all of which were warning me not to pursue an intimate relationship with Sarah. But at the time I was oblivious to this.

I got the key from the manager and finally I was in the hotel room Sarah in my arms. But almost immediately we were interrupted when the phone rang. It was the hotel manager at the front desk. She asked me to explain once more what had happened with the taxi driver. I did, and I was told that I would no longer be disturbed. Sarah and I were together and alone at last.

CHAPTER 48

When We Walked with Jesus

Let each of our actions bear fruit in accordance with our desire. Endow us with the wisdom to produce and share what each being needs to grow and flourish. Untie the tangled threads of destiny that bind us, as we release others from the entanglement of past mistakes. Do not let us be seduced by what would divert us from our true purpose, but illuminate the opportunities of the present moment. For you are the ground and the fruitful vision, the birth, power, and fulfillment, as all is gathered and made whole once again

~ From "The Lord's Prayer", Translated from Aramaic Directly to English

It was the weekend following my experience of "See Foam Green." I went to a lecture at the Unity Spiritual Center titled "When We Walked with Jesus." The presenter, a woman named Patricia, created a family tree of those who were around Jesus during his life. Later on she talked about souls and soul groups, and on a screen she showed pictures of people from the present. Using bullet points on accompanying slides, she placed these people in the time of Jesus. Many of them were people I knew from Unity Spiritual Center, and I hoped a picture of me was going to come up.

After an hour of watching pictures flash on the screen, I had to go to the restroom. But I thought to myself, "As soon as you leave, she'll show a photo of who you were in that lifetime." Finally I could wait no longer, so I went to relieve my bladder.

As I returned, sure enough a picture of me was up on the screen. I recognized it as one Sarah had taken when we'd visited Redwood National Park in Northern California. I scanned the bullet points on the slide during the last few seconds it appeared on the screen. And then it was gone. I was disappointed because I hadn't gotten the chance to read about my time spent during the era of Jesus. I had glimpsed some words on the slide, but I wasn't sure they'd applied to me. These read "Judas Iscariot" and "I committed suicide by hanging myself."

I was curious to see what else Patricia had written. The next slide was a picture of Sarah. The accompanying text said Sarah had been the mother of Judas. So she was my mother in that lifetime.

My mind was reeling. Judas, of all people! I sat patiently until Patricia finished her presentation and asked for questions. Several hands went up, and mine was one of them. When called on, I blurted out, "As Judas, I loved Jesus as my best friend!" I said that as an altar boy in church growing up, I'd felt a deep connection with Christ and with the Sunday services that honored him. Then I asked, "Sarah was my mother? Really?"

Other people began to speak. One man said Judas had indeed been the best friend of Jesus. Others shared their understandings about the relationship of Jesus and Judas. Someone said that after the last supper, Jesus had instructed Judas to tell the Romans where he was. Judas had agreed because of their friendship, and because he knew Jesus wanted to show the Romans and the world who he truly was – the son of God. Jesus was destined to die on the cross for all of humanity. But this death was too much for Judas, his best friend, so he hung himself.

I left with many thoughts swirling in my head. Later, back at home, I remembered various moments from my relationship with Sarah. Meanwhile, I thought of a vision I'd had, a mental image of a time long ago when I'd wept as two women had knelt at my feet. Then I recalled the past Sunday, when at the Spiritual Center, Uriel in his seafoam green shirt had talked about fragmenting. I'd had a sort of emotional melt-down, and two ladies had touched me before Sarah and her girlfriend Benedict came to my side.

In that moment I realized this event had happened at least once before in one of my many lifetimes.

There it was, staring me in the face. "See foam green" meant that I needed to gain awareness, to open my eyes and see. Benedict's name suggested Benedict Arnold, which in turn suggested betrayal, such as that of Jesus by Judas. Her name was there so I would make the right connections and remember what I needed to know from that lifetime. Then I recalled how, when Sarah had wiped my nose, I'd felt the presence of a mother and not a lover.

Everything began to make sense.

As these experiences flooded my mind, I knew where this deep sense of betrayal originated. It was the betrayal of the love of my best friend, Jesus. And it had devastated me so much that I'd been compelled to take my own life.

As the emotions accompanying this new awareness set in, my tears flowed and I was transported back to the time of Jesus. I also realized in how many other incarnations the same themes had been repeated. During all those lifetimes I'd carried a heavy burden for my betrayal, and now this weight was lifted from my shoulders. I was at peace and filled with love and gratitude!

I understood what the ending of this world meant in the Mayan calendar. It wasn't just an end. It was a rebirth: a new beginning of unconditional love. All the misunderstandings I'd held over countless incarnations dissolved in a moment of grace. It was the moment of awakening, the new shift in consciousness that 12/21/12 represented.

I also knew why the woman on my Jeep tour had said souls from the same soul group should not be together in this lifetime. Her meaning could be summed up by the philosopher George Santayana's famous statement: "Those who cannot remember the past are condemned to repeat it." But fortunately, I had now remembered.

I also knew why Sarah had come into my life once more. She was here to help me re-experience my former lives. Her presence had enabled me not only to recall the past, but to comprehend the divine being that I am and the love she'd represented for me – as a lover, as a mother, and in other forms – during many incarnations.

We'd shared a deep love lifetime after lifetime, and through her eyes I had seen and experienced the divine; it was revealed through our devotion to each other and through our reflection back to one another. I realized the truth of the saying, "We are spiritual beings having a human experience."

I now felt free from any co-dependence. I could now love with an open heart. And I was confident that my next relationship would involve mutual sharing and nurturing with no strings, no attachments.

CHAPTER 49

The Opening of the Heart

Keep love in your heart. A life without it is like a sunless garden when the flowers are dead.
   ~ Oscar Wilde

After my relationship ended, for a time I went through life feeling that my heart was closed. I didn't believe I would ever love again. And I'm not just speaking of romantic love, I'm speaking of friendship, too. This changed during a trip to California when I traveled along the coast from Santa Barbara to Big Sur looking for the right place to create a retreat center.

As I sat in a coffee shop one morning after my stay at Big Sur's Esalen Retreat Center, I wondered whether to spend another night in Carmel, one of the towns I'd enjoyed visiting that day, or whether to travel to Santa Cruz several hours to the north. I asked Spirit for guidance.

No sooner had I asked the question than a delivery truck drove by with big letters on its side: "SANTA CRUZ." I knew I had my answer. So I finished my tea, got into the rental car, turned on my GPS, and headed toward Santa Cruz.

As I drove along the coast the sun was shining, and I felt peaceful and content. My heart was closed to love, but I had accepted this fact and learned to live with it, perhaps as someone learns to live with a disability.

When I got to Santa Cruz, the weather changed. Clouds covered the sky, and the rain poured down as I drove the final miles into town. My GPS led me into the city limits, and it dropped me off just a few blocks from the main drag. As I rounded the first corner, in front of me on the side of a building was a huge sign that said "Gabriella's." I was ready for lunch, so I decided to see what lay in store for me at Gabriella's Restaurant.

I was greeted by a seating host who led me to a table between a group of four people and pair of attractive women who were chatting. I ordered a pizza and, waiting for lunch to arrive, I noticed that one of the two women was an attractive blond. Being right beside them, I couldn't help but overhear their conversation. She was confidently talking about her ex-husband and the things she'd learned during her marriage. She sounded really grounded, and I wanted to talk with her.

When my pizza arrived she looked at me and remarked, "That pizza looks great!" So I grabbed a piece off of my plate and handed it to her. Of course she refused several times and then graciously accepted my offer.

The two women began asking me questions about whether I lived there. I told them no, I was on a spiritual quest looking for my next home. They were intrigued, and I was happy to talk to them. We spoke for half an hour, and during this time I felt my heart open for the first time since my relationship had ended. I felt that I wanted to get to know the blond woman better. I could even envision a possible relationship with her.

Finally, it was time to go, and they both reached out to shake my hand. They said, "It was a pleasure meeting and talking with you," and I said the same. And off they went – never to be seen by me again (at least, not in this lifetime!).

The next morning I realized that God had placed another angel in my path.

I drove back to Los Angeles for my flight home with a big smile on my face. I knew I'd probably never get a chance to talk to the blond woman again, but I also knew deep inside my heart that I might love again. I smiled all the way home.

– THE END –

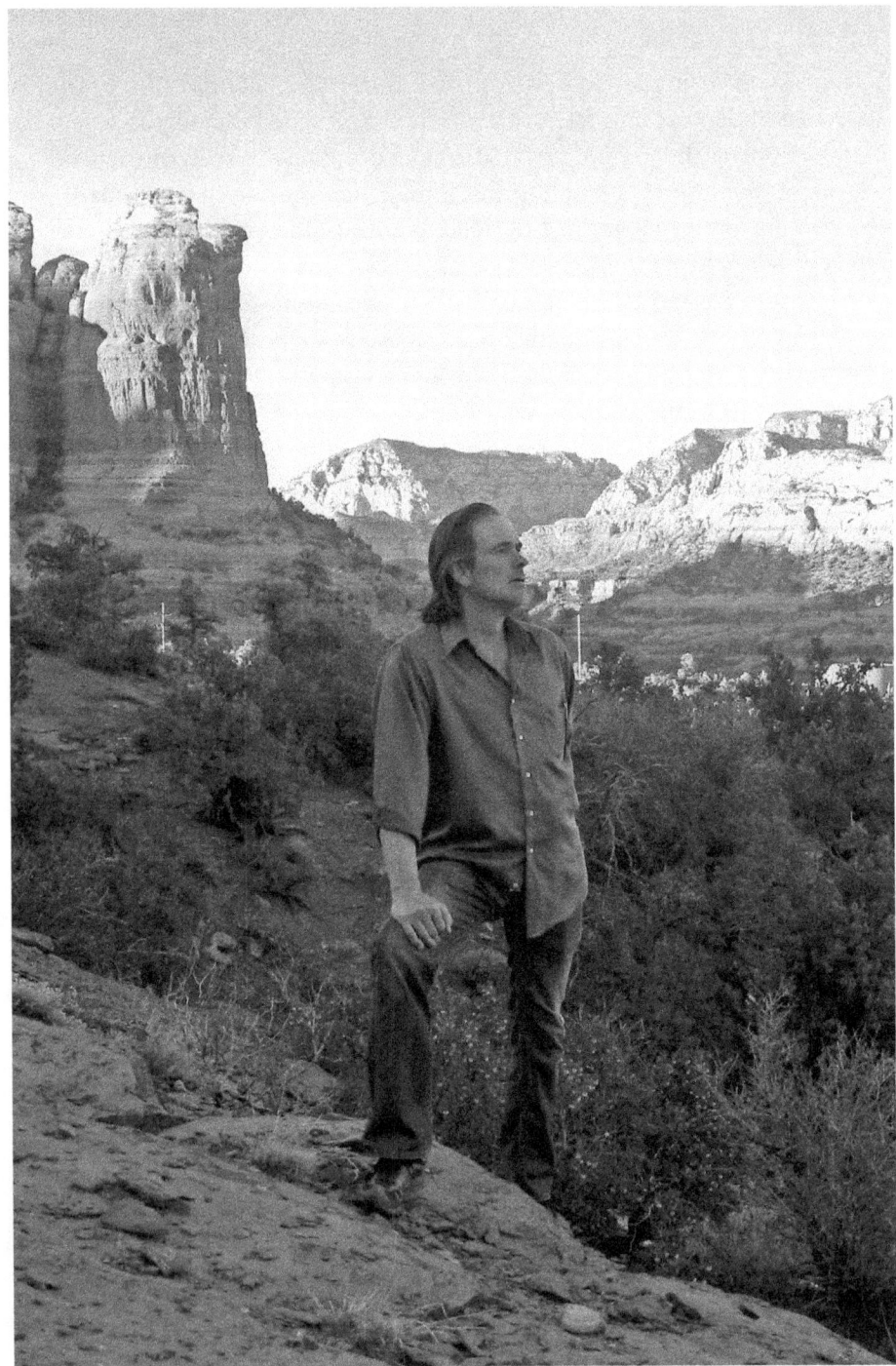

Afterword

So where am I today?

First, I'm writing another book, a sequel to this one entitled *See*.

I'm also scheduling workshops for groups, and coaching and counseling sessions for individuals, and I feel very grateful for each opportunity to help others.

My master's degree is in spiritual psychology, and my healing philosophy involves helping individuals to "get out of their own way," to release, forgive, and see the wisdom in everything we've been carrying so far. I believe that in so doing, we honor the divine soul within and we achieve true freedom.

For more information, or to schedule a session, please contact me via my website: www.trustpatiencesurrender.com.

www.ingramcontent.com/pod-product-compliance
Lightning Source LLC
Chambersburg PA
CBHW021824090426
42811CB00032B/2010/J